| PROJECT | PAGE NUMBER |

**Each project has an equipment list. Key pieces of equipment are referenced with a supplier code.
This can be cross referenced to the manufacturer in the back of the book
(For Example. "Rocket Cookie Cutter (BSA)" = Blossom Sugar Art**

It's A Dog-Eat-Dog World!

Easy

YOU WILL NEED

- One large and six mini, shop-bought swiss rolls
- 1.350g of white sugarpaste
- ProGel® Cream, Red, Pink, Black, Terracotta, Bright Green and Brown*
- Sprinkles- Metallic Bronze Sparkling Sugar Crystals* - 2 Pots
- 500g of Chocolate buttercream
- 2, 14 inch (35cm) x 12 inch (30cm) cake drums
- Heart cutter's (we used a 75mm and 40mm) you need it big enough to cover the end of your swiss roll (see Fig 5)
- Small oval cutter in three different sizes for the eyes and tongue.
- ½ batch of cookie dough (see recipe section at back of book)
- Small cel stick
- A few pieces of dried spaghetti
- Edible glue*
- Small glue brush
- Dresden tool
- 1.5m of Green 25mm ribbon

* Rainbow Dust Colour products

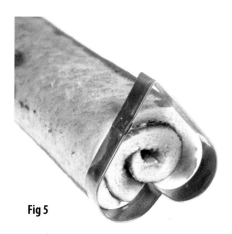

Fig 5

METHOD

1. Take the two cake drums and secure together using royal icing or a glue gun.

2. Colour 750g of white sugarpaste using bright green ProGel®. Roll out, cover the cake drum and leave to dry.

3. Trace and cut out the Sausage Dog face templates from the back of this book. Roll out the cookie dough, cut one large face and six small faces, place onto a baking tray and cook for the required time. Leave to cool completely.

4. Colour 100g white sugarpaste using the cream ProGel®. Roll and cut out a 75mm heart, attach to the cookie, point end up, using edible glue (Fig 1). Mark the whiskers with the cel stick. With the remaining sugarpaste, colour the ears, feet and tail, with a mixture of brown and terracotta ProGel®, until the desired colour is achieved.

5. For the ears, roll out and cut two 40mm heart shapes. Cut one in half and attach each piece to the cookie using edible glue (Fig 2). Cut the second heart in half and cut a thin strip from the centre (Fig 3) and attach this to the first piece of ear (Fig 4). Brush a small amount of edible glue onto the crescent of the ear and attach the metallic bronze sugar crystals as shown in the main image on the opposite page.

6. To make the eyes, use the larger of the oval cutters, cut two cream eyes and using the small oval cutter, cut out two black centres . Attach the centres in place with edible glue.

7. Using the large oval cutter, cut out a pink tongue, cutting off the top quarter and mark a line down the centre. Secure in place with edible glue. Form a small ball for the nose, attach in place and leave to dry.

8. For the dogs bodies, cover the whole swiss roll with chocolate butter cream, leaving one end exposed. Cover the buttercream with metallic bronze sugar crystals and place onto the covered cake board. Place the face cookie onto the body using a small amount of buttercream.

9. To make the tail, use the remaining brown sugarpaste. Roll a ball into a long cone shape, push in a piece of dried spaghetti and attach to the dog. For the feet, make four bigger cones, mark the toes using the dresden tool and place in position on the dog.

10. Make 6 small puppies using the above techniques and the smaller set of cutters.

11. Decorate the board with a selection of sugar flowers.

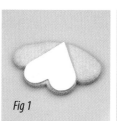

Fig 1

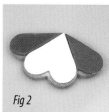

Fig 2

Fig 3

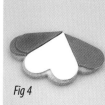

Fig 4

TO MAKE DOG COLLAR COOKIES

YOU WILL NEED (MAKES 12)

- 1/2 batch of cookie dough (recipe in back of book)
- 500g of white sugarpaste
- 150g of white flowerpaste
- ProGel®* in a selection of colours (we used Grey, Orange, Pink, Yellow, Purple and Turquoise).
- Edible Glue*
- Click-Twist Brush® - Dark Metallic Silver
- Edible Silk Range - Metallic Light Silver*
- Edible Food Pen - Black*
- 90mm, 55mm, 8mm, and 5mm round circle cutters
- Dog bone template - See back of book

*Rainbow Dust Colour products

METHOD

1. Roll out the cookie dough to approx 5mm. Cut out circles using a 90mm circle cutter and place onto a greased baking tray. Using a 55mm circle cutter, take out the centre. Bake for the required time and leave to cool completely.

2. While the cookie's are cooling, colour all of the white flowerpaste with a small amount of grey ProGel® to make the studs and dog tag. Cut out five 8mm circle's and five 5mm circle's for each collar. Using a small amount of edible glue, attach the small circle on the top of the large circle and leave to dry.

3. Roll out and cut the bone shaped dog tag's out of the grey flowerpaste using the template and leave to dry. Once dry, the studs can be painted using a metallic dark silver Click-Twist Brush®. The dog tag's can be dusted with edible silk, metallic light silver.

4. Divide the white sugarpaste into 12 and colour each one using any colours from the ProGel® range. Roll out and cut a large 90mm circle from the sugarpaste and brush a small amount of edible glue onto the cookies surface.

5. Place the sugarpaste onto the cookie and using the smaller 55mm cutter cut out the centre piece of paste. Once your have completed your collars in the colours of your choice, you can attach the studs and dog tag with a small amount of edible glue. Write the name of each guest onto the tag with a black edible food pen.

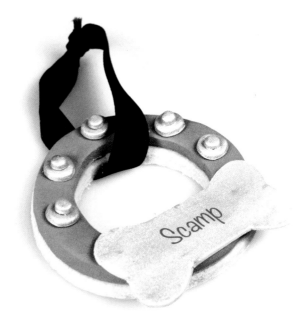

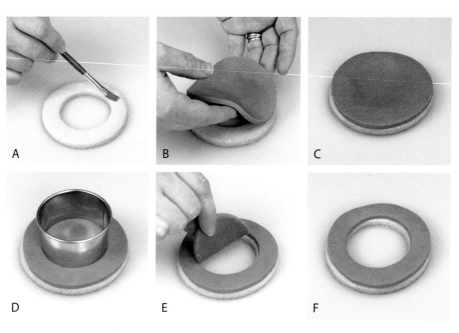

A

B

C

D

E

F

Just Add Glitter!

Medium

YOU WILL NEED

- 6 inch (15cm) round cake
- 8 inch (20cm) round cake
- 10 inch (25.5cm) round cake
- 4 x 8 inch (20cm) round cake drums
- 16 inch (40.5cm) round cake drum
- 3kg of white sugarpaste
- Dark Gold Metallic Food Paint* x 2
- EasyCover Sponge*
- Sparkle Range (Non-Toxic Glitter)*- Jewel Lilac
- Craft Dust Range*- Frosted Orchid
- Edible Glitter*- Purple
- Edible Glue*
- Dowels
- Confectioners varnish
- Trex (or white vegetable fat)
- Stencil of your choice
- White peace roses, approx 40 (small 55mm)
- 4m purple 15mm satin ribbon
- 1m gold 15mm satin ribbon
- Royal Icing
- Small paint brush
- Dipping solution*
- Tilting turntable
- 4 inch (10cm) round dummy cut to a depth of approx 2.5in (6.5cm)
- 4 inch (10cm) thin cake card

FOR THE CUPCAKES

- Large cupcakes baked in gold cases
- Multi rose mould (FPC)
- Rose cake wrappers
- The Sparkle Range - Jewel Lilac*
- ProGel®*- Purple
- 100g of white flowerpaste (for 6 cakes)
- 300g of white sugarpaste (for 6 cakes)
- Circle cutter the same size as your cupcake

   * Rainbow Dust Colour products

METHOD

1. Place the 6 inch cake on the 8 inch drum board and cover the cake and the board with white sugarpaste. Repeat with the 10 inch cake and the 16 inch board.

2. Secure together the 3, 8 inch drum boards with royal icing. Sit the 8 inch cake on top of the drum boards and place on a spare board. Cover with white sugarpaste, trimming neatly around the base of the cake. Leave all the cakes to dry and firm overnight.

3. Using a slightly damp EasyCover sponge, dip it into the metallic food paint and dab all over the cakes until they are completely covered. (Depending on the colour of paint used, the first coat of paint can sometimes look patchy.) Leave the cakes to dry overnight then repeat the process once more.

4. Mix the confectioners varnish with the frosted orchid craft dust until a paint consistency is achieved. Paint all the roses and leave to dry.

5. Using a small paint brush and the edible glue, paint around the edge of each petal and sprinkle with the jewel lilac*. Shake off the excess glitter and repeat with the remaining roses.

6. Place the middle tier onto the tilting turntable and tilt the cake so it is leaning as far back as possible. Place the stencil along the front of the cake, leaving enough space at the base to attach the purple, 15mm ribbon and using the trex, rub into all the spaces of the stencil. Apply the edible glitter by sprinkling over the trex. Using your finger, rub the glitter into the trex until the gaps are fully covered. Lift the stencil off the cake very carefully and repeat around the remaining sides.

7. Dowel the base tier and attach the middle tier on top with a little royal icing over the dowels. Place the 4 inch cake card in the centre of the middle tier and mark around the edge. Dowel in the marked area, attach the thin card to the dummy with royal icing and then place on top of the dowels.

8. Do not attach the top tier to the dummy, as this can be assembled at the venue. To ensure that the roses fit correctly into the space, place the top tier on the dummy separator and attach the roses within the space created. Secure the roses with a little royal icing. Lift the top tier off the separator and attach the gold ribbon around the board.

9. Attach the purple ribbon onto the boards and cakes as pictured. Secure the roses around the base of the cake. To finish the top tier, place a small mound of sugarpaste in the centre of the cake and attach 4 roses around the edge of the mound and one in the centre.

CUPCAKES

1. Paint the cupcake wrappers using the metallic dark gold food paint. Colour the white flowerpaste using the purple ProGel®*and make one large rose for each cupcake (push the sugarpaste firmly into the mould, lifting out using a cocktail stick or scriber). Before the rose has dried, sprinkle with the jewel lilac glitter, shake off any excess and leave to to dry.

2. Roll out the white sugarpaste and cut out a circle to fit on the top of the cupcake. Then, using the EasyCover sponge, paint the circle and place on top of the cupcake. Attach a rose in the centre of the cupcake and finish by placing the cakes into the gold wrappers.

A Bun In The Oven

Medium

YOU WILL NEED
(CHRISTENING CAKE, CUPCAKE TOWER)

- 23 cupcakes in pink cases
- 400g of white sugarpaste
- 20g of white flowerpaste
- ProGel®* Pink
- Edible Silk Range* Pearl White
- Metallic Food paint* Pearlescent Pink
- Edible Glitter - Ivory*
- Edible Glue*
- Quilting embosser (PWC)
- Baby shoe moulds (FPC)
- 50mm 5 petal cutter
- 30mm 5 petal cutter
- Medium 10mm Blossom plunger
- Large 13mm Blossom plunger
- Scriber
- A batch of buttercream
- Plain end nozzle - 12mm
- Royal Icing (in a piping bag with a No. 2 tube)
- EasyCover sponge*
- Cupcake Stand (our choice of stand held 23 cupcakes)

* Rainbow Dust Colour products

METHOD

CUPCAKES WITH SHOES

1. Using the white flowerpaste and baby show mould, make the pairs of shoes and straps. Attach the straps to the shoes and leave to dry.

2. Colour a small amount of white flowerpaste using pink ProGel®. Using the 10mm blossom plunger cutter, make one blossom for each shoe.

3. Trim the tops off the cupcakes to make them level and spread with a thin layer of buttercream.

4. Cut out discs of white sugarpaste the same size as the top of the cupcakes and place on the top of the cakes. Paint with the pearlescent pink food paint using the Easy cover sponge and leave to dry.

5. Dust the shoes with edible silk, pearl white and paint the insides of

the shoes with pearlescent pink food paint. Attach a pink blossom to the end of the strap.

6. Attach the shoes to the top of the cupcakes with a small amount of royal icing.

CUPCAKES WITH LARGE FLOWER

1. To make the large flower, using a small amount of white flowerpaste, cut out one 50mm, one 30mm 5 petal flower, and one 13mm blossom. Attach the flowers together using edible glue and place in a flower former to dry. When dry, paint with pearlescent pink food paint and leave to dry once again.

2. Using a plain end nozzle, pipe a swirl of buttercream onto the cupcakes and sprinkle with the edible ivory glitter. Place a large flower onto each cake.

QUILTED CUPCAKES

1. Using the medium blossom plunger and the white flowerpaste cut out blossoms and leave to dry. Paint each blossom with pearlescent pink food paint. Level the tops of the cupcakes and spread with a thin layer of buttercream.

2. Roll out the white sugarpaste and emboss using the quilting embosser. Cut out discs the same size as the top of the cakes and secure in place.

3. Dust the top of the cakes with edible silk, pearl white and attach the pink blossoms with a small dot of royal icing alternately on the quilting design.

BUTTERCREAM SWIRL CUPCAKES WITH BLOSSOMS

1. Using flowerpaste, make a selection of different sized blossoms, and leave to dry. Paint with pearlescent pink food paint and leave to dry.

2. Colour the buttercream using the pink ProGel®*and pipe a swirl onto the cupcakes using a plain end nozzle. Arrange the blossoms over the swirls.

YOU WILL NEED (BLOSSOM COOKIES, MAKES 12)

- 500g of white sugarpaste
- 1/2 batch of cookie dough (see recipe at back of book)
- Edible Glitter - Ivory*
- Edible Glue*
- Double-Sided blossom cutter/scallop cutter (FMM)
- 90mm - 6 petal cookie cutter
- X-Large 25mm blossom plunger cutter
- Medium 10mm blossom plunger cutter
- Edible Silk - Pearl White*
- Royal Icing in a piping bag with a No. 2 tube
- ProGel® - Pink

METHOD

1. Using the 90mm petal cutter, cut out and bake 12 cookies (as per recipe) and leave to cool.

2. Roll out the white sugarpaste and cut out 12 x 90mm petals and attach to each cookie using the edible glue. Once secure, brush lightly with the edible silk, pearl white.

3. Cut out 12, X-large petals from the sugarpaste and set aside.

4. Colour the remaining sugarpaste using the pink ProGel®. Roll out and cut 12 Blossoms using the double-sided cutter (FMM) and 12 10mm blossoms.

5. Brush the large pink blossoms with edible silk, pearl white and attach to the cookie. Brush the X-large blossoms with edible glue, sprinkle them with Ivory edible glitter and attach to the cookie. Attach one of the small blossoms (which has been dusted with pearl white) and finish the centre with a dot of royal icing.

6. To finish, pipe small dots around the edge of each cookie.

Baby It's A Rich Mans World

YOU WILL NEED

- Edible Silk Range - Metallic Morrocan Velvet and Metallic Ginger Glow*
- Dark Chocolate Vermicelli*
- Polystyrene cone
- Chocolate shot glasses
- 1kg of Belgian milk chocolate
- Large slipper mould
- Butterfly trio mould
- Mini cake cases

* Rainbow Dust Colour products

METHOD - TRUFFLE TOWER

1. Make a batch of your favourite truffles, (or use ready-made ones) dip each one into tempered chocolate (see recipe section at back of book) and leave to set. Once set, they can be brushed with the edible silk lustre powder. Cover the cone with melted chocolate and leave to set. The truffles can be attached to the cone with a small amount of melted chocolate.

METHOD - CHOCOLATE SHOT GLASSES

2. Take a plastic shot glass and highly polish the inside with kitchen roll before adding the chocolate, this will give the chocolate a high gloss finish. Take the plastic shot glass and fill with tempered chocolate, then pour out and to leave to set. Repeat once more in the same shot glass to build up a second coat of chocolate. Once completely set, the chocolate will have shrunk from the sides of the shot glass, allowing it to be easily removed. It can then be brushed with metallic ginger glow.

METHOD - SHOES

1. Polish the slipper mould with kitchen roll, pour tempered chocolate into the mould, making sure the shoe is completely coated. Leave to set and add a second layer of chocolate for added strength. Once set, remove from the mould. Using a small amount of melted chocolate, attach the 2 halves together. Don't worry if it looks a little untidy at this stage, as the chocolate can be trimmed once set. Taking a small pallet knife or craft knife, gently run the sharp edge along the seam to remove any unsightly edges. Once trimmed, it can be dusted using the edible silk, morrocan velvet and filled with truffles.

METHOD - MINI CHOCOLATE CASES

1. Make the mini chocolate cases using the same principles; pour the chocolate into the cases, swirl around and pour the excess chocolate out. Repeat to build a second layer. Once dry, dust alternately using the edible silk, moroccan velvet and the ginger glow and add truffles to the chocolate cases.

METHOD - CHOCOLATE BUTTERFLIES

1. Make the butterflies by pouring the chocolate into the mould and leaving to set. Push out carefully and lustre. Decorate the shoes and chocolate cases with the butterflies, attaching them with a small amount of melted chocolate. Finish by attaching large gold butterflies randomly spaced to the left and right of the tower as shown in the main image.

Flutter By, Butterfly!

Easy

YOU WILL NEED

- 10 inch (25.5cm) round cake covered in ivory sugarpaste
- 14 inch (35.5cm) round cake drum covered in ivory sugar paste
- 1.750kg of Ivory sugarpaste
- 300g - white flowerpaste
- Three petal & fern/leaf shape eyelet
- Deep frill cutter (JEM set of 2)
- Heart shape cutters: Top set of wings -90mm with 23mm cut out.
- Bottom set of wings -70mm with 15mm and 10mm hearts cut out.
- Circle cutters- Top and bottom wings 10mm and 6mm
- Medium butterfly plunger cutter
- Frilling Stick (JEM)
- Sprinkles* Black sugar strands
- ProGel®*- Claret, Orange, Bright Green and Black
- Edible Glitter*- Strawberry and Orange
- Metallic Food Paint*- Pearlescent Spring Green and Pearlescent Cerise.
- Sparkling Sugar Crystals - Orange and Rose
- Edible Glue*
- Medium paint brush
- Small dusting brush
- Small amount of royal icing
- 1.5m cerise, 15mm ribbon

* Rainbow Dust Colour products

METHOD

1. Cover your cake and board with Ivory sugarpaste and leave to dry. Colour equal amounts of white flowerpaste with claret, orange and bright green ProGel®*(leaving a small amount white for the eyes). Roll out the flowerpaste and using the butterfly plunger cutter, cut out 13 claret and 13 orange butterflies. Leave to dry over a piece of card which has been folded in half to create a former.

2. Using flowerpaste and the 90mm heart cutter, cut out 2 hearts in claret and 2 in orange. Using the same cutter, lower the cutter 20mm from the top of the hearts and cut, leaving only the top piece of the hearts (this is used to edge the outer wing).

3. With the remaining bottom half of the heart, use the 23mm heart cutter and the circle cutters to cut out the pattern from the wing (as shown in main image). Repeat this for both wings. Create the lower wings in the same way, using the smaller heart cutters.

4. Attach the cut out piece of wing (from point 2) to the larger plain wing with edible glue and leave all pieces the dry.

5. Roll out ivory sugarpaste and cut out the side design using the deep frill cutter. Cut out the eyelets at the top of each point and attach around the cake using edible glue.

6. Using the pearlescent spring green food paint and the small dusting brush, paint the side design using a stippling technique (see tips*). Once the butterflies are dry, paint each one with edible glue and sprinkle over the co-ordinating edible glitter. Leave to dry on the former once again.

7. To assemble the large butterfly (for the top of the cake), brush the outer wings with edible glue and sprinkle over the matching edible glitter. Repeat on the area at the top of the wings with the cut outs and leave to dry.

8. Colour a piece of sugarpaste using cerise ProGel® and roll out a long sausage for the body, making it thinner at the base and more ball like at the top for the head. Mark a mouth and leave to firm for a short while. Once firm brush with edible glue and sprinkle with the matching edible glitter.

9. Secure the body of the butterfly in the centre of the cake using edible glue. Attach the wings to the sides of the body (as shown in the main image).

10. Colour a small amount of flowerpaste using the orange ProGel®. Roll out 2 thin sausages for the butterfly's antennas and attach at the top of the head in a coil. For the eyes, roll 2 small balls of white flowerpaste, add 2 small black pupils and attach to the head. Use black sugar strands for the eye lashes. Finally attach the butterflies around the base of the cake with royal icing and write on an inscription if you wish. When dry, paint the inscription with pearlescent cerise food paint.

* TIP: STIPPLING

Load the brush with paint, then dab the brush all over the area you require covering.

If You Go Down To The Woods Today....

YOU WILL NEED

- 12 inch (30cm) square Board
- 5 inch (13cm) square thin board
- 5 inch (13cm) square cake
- 8 inch (20cm) square cake
- 2kg of Ivory sugarpaste
- 1.5kg of white sugarpaste
- 200g white flowerpaste
- Small piece of black sugarpaste (for the eyes)
- ProGel®*- Cream, Brown and Baby Blue
- Edible Silk Range*- Ivory Shimmer, Blue Shimmer and Mocha Shimmer
- Sparkle Range (Non-Toxic Glitter)*- White Hologram
- Metallic Food Paint*- Pearlescent Ivory
- EasyCover Paint Sponge*
- Edible Glue*
- Dipping Solution*
- Honeycomb texture mat
- Button mould (FPC)
- Bow maker cutters- medium and large (JEM)
- Cutting wheel
- Dowels
- Large cel stick
- Royal icing in piping bag with a No. 2 tube (you will need a No. 3 nozzle if making the large button cupcakes)
- Large dusting brush
- Frilling stick - Tool 12 (JEM) Also incorporates the "mouth" tool
- Strip cutter 50mm (JEM)
- Marzipan spacers
- 5mm circle cutter (for the teddy bear cupcakes)
- 10mm circle cutter (for the cookies)
- Tylo Powder*
- 1.5m of Brown, 15mm ribbon

* Rainbow Dust Colour products

METHOD

1. Using the Ivory Sugarpaste, cover the 5 inch cake on the thin board, trimming the base neatly. Place the 8 inch cake in the centre of the 12 inch board and cover the cake, leaving the board uncovered at this stage. Leave to dry. Dowel and stack the cakes, securing them together with a small amount of royal icing.

2. Paint the cakes using the EasyCover sponge and pearlescent ivory food paint. Leave to dry for about 2 hours. Using ProGel®, colour some of the white flowerpaste cream, baby blue and brown. Take the button maker and mould 28 large buttons in a combination of the 3 colours. You will also needs a selection of smaller buttons in cream and blue to decorate the bear. Leave to dry. Colour 500g of white sugarpaste with baby blue ProGel®, roll out into strips and cover the board around the cake. Then using the edible silk, blue shimmer and a large dusting brush, lustre the icing on the board.

3. Roll out baby blue sugarpaste, using the spacers as a guide. Emboss with the honeycomb texture mat and cut out strips long enough to fit along each side of the cake. Once they are cut to the required length, brush with edible silk, blue shimmer and attach to the cake with edible glue. Repeat the process until all sides of the cake are covered.

4. Using the cutting wheel, mark lines at equal distances along the top and bottom of each of the strip.

5. Colour white flowerpaste using the baby blue ProGel®, roll out thinly and emboss with the honeycomb texture mat. Using the large bow cutter, cut out 8 sets of bows and tails. Make each bow and leave to dry. While the tails are still soft, brush each tail with white hologram glitter (which has been mixed with a little dipping solution to create a glitter paint).

6. Attach 2 tails to all corners of the cake with edible glue. Once the bows are dry, brush with the white hologram glitter in the same way as the tails. Attach the bows to the top of the tails using royal icing.

7. Brush all the buttons in the co-ordinating edible silk lustres and using royal icing in the piping bag with a No. 2 tube, mark the cotton on the button. Attach the large buttons to the cake with royal icing, 4 buttons on the base panels and 3 on the top panels.

TEDDY BEAR

1. Colour 375g of the white sugarpaste with brown ProGel®, adding a little Tylo powder to firm the paste slightly. Using 190g of this paste, form an egg shape for the body, marking a line down the centre, back and sides using the stitching wheel. Use 30g for each leg and form into a tapered sausage shape, moulding a foot at the thicker end. Mark round the end of the of the foot and down the side of the leg with the stitching wheel, repeat with the other leg and attach to the side of the body with edible glue*.

2. Using 25g for each arm, form into a cone and slightly flatten. Mark stitching down the sides of the arm and attach to the side of the teddy with edible glue*.

3. To Make the head, use 70g of brown sugarpaste and form into a ball. Using your fingers, gently press around the top half of the ball back and forth, to form the muzzle. Slightly flatten the top half and push the bottom half out to form the cheeks, adding detail using the stitching wheel. Mark a mouth and eyes using the cel stick and attach to the teddy with edible glue and a wooden skewer (or piece of dried spaghetti) inserted all the way through the bear.

4. With the remaining brown sugarpaste, make 2 small balls for the ears. Using the larger end of the cel stick, create an indentation in the ball to resemble the inside of the ear. Attach to the head with edible glue. Leave to dry.

5. Once dry lustre the bear with edible silk, mocha shimmer. Attach the small buttons (made in point 2) to the bear, adding a larger blue button to the bears tummy. Make a nose out of a small piece of cream flowerpaste and pipe royal icing into the eye sockets, finishing with a tiny ball of black sugarpaste at the base of the eye. Attach to the top of the cake using royal icing.

TEDDY BEAR CUPCAKES

Make the small teddy bears in the same way as the large teddy bear, using a total of 85g of brown sugarpaste. Using 35g for the body, 5g for each arm, 5g for each leg, 25g for the head and 5g for both ears. Cut tiny circles for the buttons using a 5mm circle cutter. Leave to dry before placing them onto the cupcake. Cut the top off the cupcake to make it level and cover with a disc of cream sugarpaste, lustred with edible silk ivory shimmer. Attach the teddy bear by securing with royal icing.

LARGE BUTTON CUPCAKE

Level the tops of the cupcakes. Cut out discs of sugarpaste in cream, blue and brown, to match the top of your cupcake. Then using a slightly smaller circle cutter, mark an inner circle but do not cut through the disc. Mark the 4 holes in the middle by using the pointed end of the cel stick and use the rounded end to create a shallow hollow over each of the 4 holes. Dust each disc in co-ordinating edible silk lustre and attach to the top of your cupcake. Then using royal icing in a piping bag with a No. 3 nozzle, pipe the cotton across the holes.

BOW CUPCAKES

Using the medium bow cutter, make the bow in the same way as the main cake and dust with edible silk, blue shimmer. Trim the tops off the cupcakes to make level and cover with a disc of brown sugarpaste, dusting with edible silk, mocha shimmer. Attach the bow to the top with royal icing.

Large Button Cupcake

Teddy Bear Cupcake

Bow Cupcake

Mini Button Cupcake

BUTTON LOLLIES

Make a batch of lollies by piping discs of melted chocolate onto a sheet of parchment paper and place a stick half way onto the disc, leave to set. Make the buttons in the same way as the large button cupcakes, Making them slightly smaller to fit your lolly. Secure them onto the lolly with royal icing and finish with a bow of ribbon on each stick.

MINI BUTTON CUPCAKES

Make a selection of buttons in brown and blue and dust with edible silk lustre. Using a plain end nozzle, pipe a swirl of buttercream which has been coloured with cream ProGel and arrange the buttons on the top of the swirl.

BUTTON COOKIES

Make a batch of cookie dough (recipe at back of book) and divide into three equal parts. Leave one part plain and colour the other two with baby blue and brown ProGel®. Cut out discs using a circle cookie cutter, then using a small 10mm circle cutter, cut out four holes in the middle. Leave to rest, then bake for the required time. Once cool they can stacked in threes and threaded with ribbon and tied in a bow.

"Sparkles" Are A Girls Best Friend!

YOU WILL NEED

Please allow 3 days drying time to make the shoes and handbag

- 12 inch (30cm) Teardrop shaped cake
- 15 inch x 13 inch (38cm x 33cm) oval cake drum
- 2kg of white Sugarpaste
- 400g of white flowerpaste
- ProGel®*- Pink and Black
- Sparkle Range (Non-Toxic Glitter)*- Jewel Brilliant Pink, and Jewel Gunmetal
- Edible Silk Range*- Metallic Dark Silver and Pearl Blush Pink.
- Edible Glue*
- Large and small wedding slipper mould
- Templates for handbags & shoe insoles - See back of book
- Circle cutters- 60mm, 30mm, 25mm,20mm, 15mm and 10mm.
- 2m of 40mm dusky pink satin ribbon
- 2m of 15mm black satin ribbon
- Small piece of 25mm black satin ribbon
- Large dusting brush
- Craft knife
- Cutting wheel
- Cel pad
- Trex, Cornflour, Royal icing

* Rainbow Dust Colour products

METHOD

1. Colour the white sugarpaste using the black ProGel® and cover both the cake and board. Colour 250g of white flowerpaste using the pink ProGel®, adding a small amount of trex to make it easier to work with. Grease the large slipper mould with trex and dust over with a small amount of cornflour. This will stop your shoe from sticking in the mould.

2. Roll out the pink flowerpaste to approx. 5mm and press carefully into the shoe mould. Trim off any excess paste using the craft knife (dipping the craft knife into trex will stop the knife dragging through the flower paste and causing creases). Repeat the same process with the other half of the shoe and leave to dry until firm enough to handle.

3. The shoe halves can now be carefully taken out of the mould and left to finish drying overnight on a cel pad. Repeat this method to make the other full shoe. Make the small slippers using the same method.

4. To make the handbags, trace and cut out the template from the back of the book. Using the pink flowerpaste, roll out to approx. 5mm thick and cut out 2 pieces for the front and back of the bag. Leave to dry on a cel pad (the sides will be made at the assembly stage). Repeat this process for the small handbags using the black flowerpaste.

5. To make the large handles, use black flowerpaste and cut out 2 x 60mm circles. Remove a 30mm circle from the middle, off centre and leave to dry.

6. To make the small handles use pink flowerpaste cut out 2x 25mm circles. Remove a 10mm circle from the middle, off centre. Leave to dry.

7. To make the shoe decoration, use grey flowerpaste and cut out 2 x 30mm circles. Remove a 15mm circle from the middle, off centre. Using pink flowerpaste, cut out 5 x 20mm circles, remove a 10mm circle from the middle, off centre. Leave to dry.

8. To assemble the shoes, soften down a small ball of pink flowerpaste by mixing in edible glue until you have a smooth, thick, sticky paste. Apply this paste around the edges of the shoe. Attach the two halves together, making sure there is enough paste on the shoes to form a secure bond. Don't worry if it looks messy at this stage. Assemble all the shoes in the same way and leave to dry. Once dry, the excess paste can be trimmed from the seams using a craft knife, leaving a smooth neat shoe. Repeat with all shoes.

9. Using the dusting brush, paint the outside of the shoe with edible glue (including the heel). Cover with glitter, shaking off any excess and leave to dry. Repeat this method with all the shoes (we used jewel brilliant pink and Jewel gunmetal). Using the shoe insole template (from the back of the book), cut out black insoles for the large shoes and dust using the edible silk, metallic dark silver. Dust the pink insoles with edible silk, pearl blush pink. Cover all the bag handles and shoe decoration circles in the same way.

10. Assemble the bag by cutting out the 2 side panels (template in back of book), approx 5mm thick from pink flowerpaste. Using edible glue, apply to the outer edges of one of the large pieces of the handbag. Attach the side panels and support (use sponge pieces as support). Apply glue around the edge of the remaining half of the bag. Place this on the top of the side pieces. Once you are happy with the assembly and it has been left to firm for about half an hour, carefully stand the bag upright and leave to dry.

11. Once dry, roll out a piece of pink flowerpaste, larger than the bottom of the bag. Glue the bottom edges of the bag and place on top of the flowerpaste, trimming around the bag with a cutting wheel to create the base. Leave to dry.

12. Glitter the bag using the same technique as the shoes. Attach the handles with a small amount of royal icing and repeat with the small handbag. Attach the shoe decorations to the shoe toes with royal icing, over lapping two sizes of different colours.

13. Finish by attaching the dusky pink ribbon around the cake, securing with a single dot of royal icing where the ribbon ends meet. Make a bow and attach a pink glittered circle in the centre of the bow and secure to the front side of the cake. Place the shoes and handbags on the cake, securing with royal icing. To finish, attach the black ribbon around the board using a glue stick.

Glad Rags
& Handbags

YOU WILL NEED (MAKES 6 CUPCAKES)

- Six cupcakes in the flavour of your choice.
- 550g of white sugarpaste
- 50g of white flowerpaste
- Tylo Powder*
- Edible Glue*
- ProGel®*- Pink and Black.
- Edible Silk range*- Metallic Dark Silver and Pearl Blush Pink.
- Sparkle Range (Non-Toxic Glitter)*- Jewel Brilliant Pink and Jewel Gun Metal.
- FPC- 3D Handbag mould
- Circle cutters- 20mm,15mm,10mm and 5mm.
- Trex.
- Dusting Brush
- Royal icing

    * Rainbow Dust Colour products

METHOD

1. Divide the white flowerpaste in half and colour one half pink and one half black using the ProGel®* food colour.

2. Using a small amount of black flowerpaste, roll out and cut 3 x 20mm circles, removing a 15mm circle from the middle, off centre. Then using the pink flowerpaste, cut 6 x 10mm circles removing a 5mm circle from the middle, off centre. Once dry brush with edible glue and sprinkle over the matching glitter.

3. Divide the white sugarpaste in half and colour equal amounts pink and black using the ProGel®. You will need approximately 125g pink and 125g black sugarpaste to cover the cupcakes. With the remainder, add Tylo Powder to your paste until it starts to firm. Add a small amount of trex into the sugarpaste, this will make it nice and soft and much easier to use with the moulds. Rub a small amount of trex into the mould and firmly press in the sugarpaste, cutting off any excess to make a flat top. Push out carefully. Repeat the process

with the other half and glue together using edible glue. Repeat this process again for the black bags and leave to dry. Dust the pink and black bags with edible silk, pearl blush pink and metallic dark silver.

4. Attach the handles to the bags with royal icing.

5. Roll out the remaining coloured sugarpaste and using a round cutter, cut out 3 discs of each colour to cover the tops of your cupcakes. Finish each top with the co-ordinating edible silk, lustre. Take the disc and place on top of the cupcake, attaching with a small amount of buttercream if you wish (level your cupcake first, if required).

6. To finish, add a bag to each cupcake, securing with royal icing.

Put On Your Dancing Shoes!

YOUR WILL NEED (MAKES 6 SHOE COOKIES)

- Batch of cookie dough (recipe at back of book)
- Edible Silk Range* - Metallic Dark Silver and Pearl Blush Pink
- Sparkle Range (Non-Toxic Glitter)* Jewel Gunmetal and Jewel Brilliant Pink
- ProGel®*- Pink and Black
- Circle cutters- 30mm and 15mm
- Shoe cutter.
- 100g White flowerpaste
- 300g White sugarpaste
- Edible Glue*
- Royal icing
- Dusting brush
- Side design embosser (we used the Stephen Benison lattice side design roller) or any embosser of your choice.

   * Rainbow Dust Colour products

METHOD

1. Cut out 6 shoes from the cookie dough, place onto a baking tray and bake for the required time. Leave to cool.

2. Colour a small amount of the white flowerpaste pink and black using the ProGel® colours. Roll out and cut 6 x 30mm circles from each colour, removing a 15mm circle from the middle, off centre. Once dry, brush with edible glue, sprinkle over the co-ordinating glitter and leave to dry.

3. Colour white sugarpaste pink and black using the ProGel® colours (enough to cover 6 cookies). Roll, emboss and cut out the shoe shape, trimming off the heel at an angle (see picture). Roll and cut out another shoe without embossing, cut off and retain the heel. Attach these pieces to the cookie with edible glue. Make 5 more shoes. Once complete, brush each cookie in the co-ordinating edible silk lustre.

4. Attach the glittered circles for the toe decoration with royal icing. Attach the large pink circle onto the black shoe with the smaller black circle on top. Repeat for the remaining shoes.

Fit For A Fairy Princess

Medium

YOU WILL NEED

- 8 inch (20cm) round cake
- 12 inch (30.5cm) round drum board
- 1.5kg white sugarpaste
- 200g white flowerpaste
- 200g white Mexican Modelling Paste
- Trex
- Cornflour
- ProGel®*- Cream, Mint Green, Pink, Yellow, Peach and Strawberry.
- Daisy/Gerbra plunger cutter- 70mm
- Strip cutter- hearts and blossom (FMM, set 8-12)
- Cutting wheel
- Scriber
- Frilling stick (JEM, tool 12)
- Small paintbrush
- Butterfly cookie cutter (approx 75mm)
- Heart cutter -15mm
- Circle Cutter- 25mm and 4mm cutter (or use the end of a plain nozzle) for mushroom spots
- 100mm Sphere mould- one half filled with Rice Krispie cake mix (SW)
- Wooden skewer or piece of dried spaghetti
- 5 in 1 Head Mould (KD)
- Edible Glue*
- Metallic Food Paint*- Pearlescent Spring Green and Pearlescent Cerise.
- Edible Glitter*- Cerise
- Plain and Simple Range*- Snowdrift, Black Magic.
- Sparkle Range (Non-Toxic Glitter)*- White Hologram
- Edible Silk Range*- Pearl White and Pearl Blush Pink
- Tylo Powder*
- Dipping Solution*
- Royal Icing

* Rainbow Dust Colour products

METHOD

1. Colour 1.25kg of white sugarpaste using the cream ProGel®, and cover the cake and board. Leave to dry.

2. Make a rice krispie cake (as per recipe in back of book) in one half of the sphere mould.

3. Colour 100g of white flowerpaste using the mint green ProGel®*. Roll the paste out thinly onto trex, lift off and dust the area with cornflour. Place back onto the board and using the heart strip cutter press down firmly and move the cutter about on the board (this will create a neat result). Cut along the edge of the cutter with the cutting wheel to give a straight edge. Pick out the heart centres with the scriber tool, remove the flowerpaste from the cutter and attach to the side of the cake with edible glue. Repeat this design around the base of the cake and its board (as in the main image).

4. Colour a small amount of white flowerpaste with pink ProGel®. Roll and cut out the side design again, this time retaining the hearts (you will need one heart for each space on the side and board design). Using the blossom strip cutter, cut out and retain 14 blossoms. Leave all pieces to dry. Brush with edible glue and cover with cerise edible glitter and leave to dry.

5. Paint the board and side design using pearlescent spring green paint and leave to dry. Then insert the small glittered hearts to the design using edible glue.

6. Using white flowerpaste, roll out to approx 3mm and cut out a butterfly using the cookie cutter. Cut out 2 hearts in each side of the wing using the two smaller heart cutters and leave to dry over a piece of cardboard folded in half, to make a former.

7. Colour some white sugarpaste pale green using the mint green ProGel®*. Roll out and cover the top of the cake, using a 7 inch (18cm) round board as a guide. Attach to the top of the cake using edible glue.

8. Colour 100g of white sugarpaste using the strawberry ProGel® and cover the half sphere krispie cake, leave to dry.

9. To make the mushroom stalk, add a small amount of tylo powder to 130g of white sugarpaste until the paste feels firm. Roll into a short, fat cylindrical shape to create the stalk.

10. Once both pieces are dry, attach together using royal icing. Using white flowerpaste, roll and cut out 6 large circles. Brush each circle with edible glue and sprinkle with white hologram glitter. Arrange on the toadstool and secure with edible glue.

11. Make 2 small toadstools using sugarpaste.

12. To make the fairy, take 80g of white Mexican modelling paste, colour 40g with peach ProGel® and 40g with pink ProGel®. Using 15g of peach, roll into a long sausage to make the legs, then fold in half and attach over the edge of the cake using edible glue. Fold one leg over the other and pinching the ends of the leg to form the feet.

13. Using a small amount of pink modelling paste, roll and cut out two hearts, attach to the feet with the pointed end down to make the shoes.

14. To make the dress, take 20g of pink modelling paste, cut out two daisy/gerbra flowers with the plunger cutter and using the frilling stick, frill the edge of each petal. Attach each flower onto the legs of the fairy with edible glue, overlapping the petals.

15. With the remaining 20g of pink modelling paste, mould the body by rolling into a small thick sausage, slightly thinner at one end. Indent across the top with a large cel stick to make a channel for the arms to sit.

16. Use 10g of peach modelling paste rolled into a sausage, slightly shaped at the ends to make the hands. Place the arms over the indentation at the top of the body, securing with edible glue.

17. To make the head, take the remaining 15g of peach modelling paste and use the forth largest head in the mould. Paint the eyes by mixing plain & simple, snowdrift with dipping solution and paint both the ovals of the eyes. Then using plain & simple, black magic mixed with dipping solution, paint the lower quarter of the eyes. Dust the cheeks with edible silk, pearl blush pink and attach a nose made from a tiny piece of peach paste.

18. Using the skewer, push it all the way through the centre of the fairy and through the cake until it hits the board, leaving enough exposed to attach the head. Decorate the top of the fairy's dress with small pink hearts. Sparkle the fairy's dress with white hologram glitter (mixed with a small amount of dipping solution).

19. For the hair, colour a small amount of white sugarpaste with yellow ProGel®. Roll thin sausages into strands of different lengths and attach to the head using edible glue. Curl the hair as you go to create a style.

20. To make the wings, take a small amount of white flowerpaste, roll and cut out a 75mm butterfly. Cut a small heart out of each wing and place over a former to dry. Brush the wings with edible glue, sprinkle with white hologram glitter and attach to the fairy's back with royal icing.

21. To finish, attach a small white blossom to the ends of the shoes and decorate the cake with tufts of grass.

Behind The Mask

Please note for best results you should make the masks 2 weeks before you require them.

YOU WILL NEED (MASQUERADE CAKE)

- 5 inch (13cm) round cake
- 8 inch (20cm) round cake with 2x 8 inch drums underneath
- 11 inch (28cm) round cake
- 14 inch (36cm) round drum board
- 5 inch (13cm) round thin card
- Strip cutter No. 4 - 23mm (JEM)
- Scroll and pansy set of 4 cutters (JEM)
- 85mm 5 petal cutter (FMM)
- 90mm Lacy flower cutter (JEM)
- Roller pad (JEM)
- Fabric effect roller (JEM)
- Triangle cutter 70mm
- Rope Twists mould (HH)
- Lily Stigma mould (HH)
- Leaf Cutter & Half Daisy Cutter (SB)
- Butterfly Trio mould (FPC)
- Hearts and flowers mould (FPC)
- Blossom plunger cutters (selection of sizes)
- ProGel®*- Red, Cream and Black
- Edible Glitter*- Black and Red
- 1kg of white flowerpaste
- 4 kg white sugarpaste
- Royal icing (with No. 1 tube for cupcakes and masks)
- Edible Silk Range*- Metallic Ginger Glow
- Edible Food Paint*- Metallic Dark Gold
- Edible Glue*
- Dipping Solution*
- Sparkle Range (Non-Toxic Glitter)*- Jewel Fire Red and Jewel Penny Copper*
- Flower formers (cup style)
- Flower former (for the mask)
- Dusting brush
- Small glue brush
- EasyCover Sponge*
- Dowels
- Scriber
- Craft Knife
- Black and Red feathers
- Gold Bear Grass

* Rainbow Dust Colour products

METHOD

1. Colour 2kg of white sugarpaste using black ProGel®. Cover the 11 inch cake and board, and position the cake to the back of the board to allow you to place a mask on later. Leave to dry.

2. Colour 1.25kg of white sugarpaste using the red ProGel®. Cover the 8 inch cake on a separate board and leave to dry.

3. Colour 500g of white sugarpaste using the cream ProGel®. Cover the top tier on a separate board and leave to dry.

4. Using the EasyCover sponge, paint the top tier with metallic dark gold food paint and leave to dry. Once the all the cakes are firm and dry, they can be dowelled and stacked, setting back both the middle and top tier.

BOTTOM TIER

5. Colour 200g of flowerpaste using cream ProGel®. Roll out the flowerpaste and using the strip cutter with the roller pad, cut out 12 strips. Measure and trim each strip to fit on the side of the cake. Brush each one with edible silk, metallic ginger glow and attach them evenly around the cake using edible glue.

6. Colour the remaining sugarpaste using cream ProGel® and make approx 45 balls weighing 5g each. Leave to firm and brush with edible silk, metallic ginger glow. Place the balls around the base of the cake and secure with edible glue.

MIDDLE TIER

7. Using the rope twist mould and the cream flowerpaste, roll a thin sausage. Place and press firmly into the mould, trim off the excess paste and push out the shape. Dust with edible silk, metallic ginger glow and attach to the base of the cake with edible glue. Repeat this process around the cake.

8. Colour 300g of white flowerpaste with black ProGel®*. Roll out the paste and cut out 24 triangles and leave to firm. Brush with edible glue and sprinkle with black edible glitter, shaking off any excess. Attach the first triangle to the back of the cake with edible glue, so the base of the triangle is sitting on the top of the rope design. Attach the next triangle above the first, point to point, with the base of the triangle finishing at the top of this tier. This will create the diamond side design around the cake.

9. With a small amount of cream flowerpaste, make 12 lily stigmas using the largest mould. Attach to the centre of the red diamonds with edible glue and paint using the metallic dark gold food paint.

10. Using the rope twist mould and cream flowerpaste, repeat point 7 and attach to the top edge of the cake with edible glue.

TOP TIER

11. Using the cream flowerpaste, make enough lily stigmas to go around the base of the top tier. Attach each one with edible glue and leave to firm. Paint each shape with metallic dark gold food paint.

12. Place the scroll cutter into the roller pad, roll out the black flowerpaste and place over the cutter. Roll over the paste with your rolling pin to cut the shape, leaving the piece in the mould. Carefully tease out the shape with a scriber and leave to dry until firm. Repeat until you have approx 13 pieces. Attach all the pieces with edible glue to the side of the cake.

MAKING THE MASKS

MASK DESIGN 1

1. Trace and cut out mask template No.1 (from the back of the book). Colour 50g of flowerpaste with black ProGel®. Roll out to approx 3mm and using the template, cut out the mask with a craft knife. Place the mask over the flower former (*see Fig 5*) that has been dusted with cornflour and leave to dry.

2. To make the flower decoration, colour flowerpaste with red, black and cream ProGel®. Using the red flowerpaste, cut out an 85mm, 5 petal flower, brush with edible glue and sprinkle with red edible glitter. Shake off any excess and leave the flower to dry in a flower former.

3. Using the cream flowerpaste, cut out 2 flowers using the 90mm lacy flower cutter. Place the first flower in a former and brush the centre of the flower with edible glue, attaching the second flower so that the petals are alternate from the first flower (*see fig 2*). Leave to dry. Paint using dark gold metallic food paint.

4. Once both the red and the gold flowers are dry, apply a small amount of royal icing to the centre of the red flower and attach the gold flower on top. Leave to dry.

5. Using the black flowerpaste, roll out thinly and using the calyx cutter with the roller pad, cut out one calyx for each flower, teasing the shape from the cutter with a scriber. Brush each calyx with edible glue, sprinkle with black edible glitter and shake off any excess. Apply a small dot of royal icing in the centre of the gold flower and attach the black calyx. Leave to dry.

6. Using red flowerpaste, roll out thinly and cut out blossoms using the medium blossom plunger cutter. Cut off 4 of the petals to leave a teardrop shape (*see fig 3*). Brush with edible glue and attach the 2 petal pieces around the edge of the mask.

7. Cut out 3 blossoms using the X-large blossom plunger cutter, and 2 using the medium blossom plunger cutter. Using the jewel fire red glitter (mixed with a small amount of dipping solution), paint these flowers using a small paint brush. Secure on the mask along with a selection of large and small teardrop shaped pieces with edible glue using *fig 4* as a guide.

8. Using cream flowerpaste, cut out 6 blossoms in various sizes. Paint each one with dark gold metallic food paint and leave to dry. Paint the blossoms with jewel penny copper glitter (which has been mixed with dipping solution). Attach the gold blossoms as per image (*see fig 4*)

9. Colour a small amount of royal icing with black ProGel® and place into a bag with a No.1 tube. Pipe dots and small "S" shapes around the eyes and over the mask. Paint the piping around the eyes with dark gold metallic food paint and attach the large flowers made earlier using royal icing. (*see fig 4*).

MASK DESIGN 2

1. Trace and cut out template No.2 (from the back of the book). Colour 50g of flowerpaste with black ProGel®. Roll out to approx 3mm and using the template cut out the mask with a craft knife. Place the mask over the flower former (*see Fig 1*) that has been dusted with cornflour and leave to dry.

2. Using the butterfly mould and the black flowerpaste, make a selection of sizes and leave to dry. Roll out black flowerpaste and emboss with the textured rolling pin. Cut out 3 of the half daisies and 2 leaf shapes, making sure that the leaf cutter is turned over for the opposite side of the mask.

3. Using the hearts and flowers mould with black flowerpaste, make 1 flower blossom. Lightly brush all the decorations you have made with metallic dark gold food paint to give a distressed look and leave to dry. (*see Fig 8*)

4. Using cream flowerpaste and the largest lily stigma mould, make enough pieces to go around the edge of the mask and eyes. Secure in place with edible glue and leave to dry. Paint each piece with metallic dark gold food paint. Once dry, paint with the jewel penny copper glitter (mixed with dipping solution). Using the black royal icing in a bag with a No.1 tube, pipe tiny "Z"s all over the mask and leave to dry.

5. Secure the 3, half daisies; the first one in the top centre of the mask, with the other 2 overlapping at either side. With royal icing attach the flower blossom in the centre of the mask between the eyes and finally secure the 2 leaves under each eye. Secure the various sized butterflies with royal icing (*see Fig 6*).

MASK DESIGN 3

1. Using template 2, cut out the mask using red flowerpaste. Roll out black flowerpaste and using the double scroll cutter in the roller pad, make 2 scrolls. Cut each scroll in half. Using the same method cut out one leaf scroll and leave to dry.

2. Using cream flowerpaste and the largest section of the rope twist mould, make enough rope to fit around the outer edge of the mask and attach in place using edible glue. Secure all scrolls on the mask. (*see Fig 7*).

3. Using cream flowerpaste and the large lily stigma mould, make enough pieces to fit around the eye area and the sides of the mask. Secure all pieces in place. Once dry, paint the rope edging and the stigmas with metallic dark gold food paint. Finish with penny copper glitter (mixed with dipping solution).

4. Using black flowerpaste roll out and emboss with the fabric effect roller. Cut out 3 leaves, turn the cutter over and cut out another 4 leaves. Use the same method with the red flowerpaste, cut out 6 leaves. Brush each piece lightly with metallic dark gold food paint, securing in position on the mask with royal icing. (*see Fig 7*).

5. Mix fire red glitter with dipping solution and paint the red area of the mask. Repeat this method using black hologram glitter for the black scrolls and leaf scrolls. Attach the masks in position on the sides of the cake using flowerpaste which has been softened down to a paste with edible glue. Fix skewers behind the top mask using softened down flowerpaste for extra strength. Insert the skewers of the mask into the top tier of the cake. Push a posy pick into the cake behind the mask to hold the feathers and bear grass in place. Arrange feathers behind the masks on the bottom and middle tiers, securing with royal icing if needed.

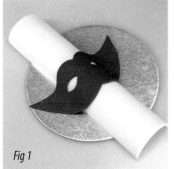

Fig 1

Fig 2

Fig 3

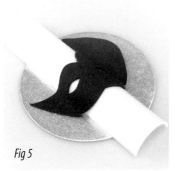

Fig 4

Fig 5

Fig 6

Fig 7

Fig 8

YOU WILL NEED (MASQUERADE CUPCAKES)

- 40mm 5 Petal cutter (FMM)
- 65mm Lacy flower cutter (OP)
- Calyx cutter (from the Strawberry Leaves and Calyx set of 4 (JEM)
- Fabric effect roller (JEM)
- Rope Twist (HH)
- Lily stigma mould (HH)
- Butterfly Trio (FPC)
- Masquerade mask mould (FPC)
- Royal Icing
- No.1 tube
- ProGel® - Red, Black and Cream *
- Edible Silk Range - Ginger Glow*
- Metallic Food Paint - Dark Gold*
- Edible Glitter - Red and Black
- Sugarpaste (approx. 35g per cake)
- Edible Glue*
- Flowerpaste
- Skewers

* Rainbow Dust Colour products

DESIGN 1

1. Cover the top of each cupcake with black sugarpaste, adding a small piece of sugarpaste underneath to create a dome. Using the cream flowerpaste and the rope twist mould, make enough rope to fit round the edge of each cupcake and secure with edible glue. Paint the rope with metallic dark gold food paint and leave to dry.

2. Make the flower in exactly the same way as "Design 1 Mask" (on the previous page), but instead, use a 40mm 5 petal cutter and a 65mm lacy flower cutter. Attach to the top of the cupcake with royal icing.

DESIGN 2

1. Cover each cupcake with red sugarpaste, creating a dome as in design 1. Using the cream flowerpaste and the largest lily stigma in the mould, make enough to go around each cupcake, attaching with edible glue. Once dry, paint with metallic dark gold food paint.

2. Using the red and black flowerpaste and the masquerade mask mould, make a mask in each colour for every cupcake. Trim a wooden skewer to approx 60mm, dip one end into edible glue, push into the side of the mask and leave to dry. You will need 2 masks for each cupcake. 1 of these mask needs to be on a skewer.

3. Using royal icing in a bag with the No.1 tube, pipe small dots around the edge and eyes of each mask. Pipe a small scroll between the forehead and eye area and leave to dry. Paint the dots and scroll using the metallic dark gold food paint.

4. For the side detail on the masks, roll out black flowerpaste, and emboss using the fabric effect roller. Using the leaf cutter, cut out 3 pieces for each cupcake with a red mask and leave to dry. Repeat with the red flowerpaste. Once all the leaves are dry, brush over very lightly using a very small amount of metallic dark gold food paint to give a distressed look. Once dry, attach 3 leaves to each mask using royal icing and a co-ordinating feather. Paint each skewer with metallic dark gold food paint and leave to dry.

5. Decorate each cupcake using one of each mask.

DESIGN 3

1. Cover each cupcake with cream sugarpaste creating the dome effect and brush each with edible silk, metallic ginger glow. Using the butterfly trio mould and black flowerpaste, make 3 medium butterflies and 14 small butterflies for each cupcake.

2. Brush each butterfly very lightly with metallic dark gold food paint to give a distressed look. Attach the small butterflies around the edge of the cupcake at different angles, using royal icing to secure in place. Leave a small area where you then need to attach a group of 3 medium butterflies.

Medium

I'd Like To Be, Under The Sea.....

Medium

YOU WILL NEED

- 7 inch (18cm) Round cake
- 12 inch (30.5cm) Round drum board
- 800g of white sugarpaste
- 400g of white flowerpaste
- 1kg of mexican modelling paste
- ProGel®* - Yellow, Green, Orange, Pink, Claret, Peach, Brown, Mint Green, Aqua and Black
- Edible Silk Range*- Irridescent Green Fusion, Irridescent Gold Fusion and Pearl Blush Pink
- Sparkle Range (Non-Toxic Glitter)* - White Hologram
- Edible Food Paint * - Metallic Dark Silver and Pearlescent Spring Green
- Dipping Solution *
- Plain and Simple Range * - Snowdrift and Black Magic
- Cel stick
- Tropical fish mould (DP)
- Seashells (FPC)
- Starfish and seashell mould (FPC)
- Formers
- Teardrop Cutter (50mm) for mermaid tail end
- Frilling stick (JEM, Tool 12)
- Small scissors
- 5 in 1 head mould (KD)
- Circle cutter (13mm)
- Circle cutter (10mm)
- Plain end cutting wheel
- Plain end piping tube No. 5
- Oval plunger cutters
- Food Pen* Black and Chocolate
- Small rose petal cutter (18mm)
- Wire cutters
- Edible Glue*
- Trex
- Cornflour
- Royal icing

* Rainbow Dust Colour products

METHOD

1. Colour 800g of white sugarpaste using aqua ProGel* (do not mix in fully as the paste needs to have a marble effect). Cover the cake and board and leave to dry.

CORAL

2. Colour a small amount of white flowerpaste using aqua, mint green, pink and orange ProGel®. Roll out each colour onto trex (lift and dust the work surface with cornflour). Using the oval plunger cutter, create holes in the flowerpaste. With the cutting wheel, cut jagged shapes out and place onto a former to dry. With any small pieces left, make into a cone shape, and using edible glue, secure in place at back. Leave these to dry upright.

LONG LEAVES

3. Roll out the flowerpaste coloured with the mint green ProGel* and with the cutting wheel, cut out long leaves freehand. Lift and twist the leaves (to give movement) and leave to dry until firm.

SHELLS

4. Using the white modelling paste, colour small amounts using yellow, green, orange, pink and aqua ProGel®. Push and press out shapes using the tropical fish and shell moulds. Make enough of the various colours for your cake. Once dry lustre using the edible silk, irridescent green fusion and gold fusion, painting some with metallic dark silver food paint for a different effect.

ROCKS

5. Colour approx 100g of white modelling paste using the black ProGel®, but do not mix in fully as the paste needs to have a marble effect. Make small and medium rocks by rolling into a ball and pinch slightly.

CORAL FLOWERS

6. Using the white modelling paste, colour small amounts using pink, yellow, orange and mint green ProGel®. Make a small ball and roll into a cone. Push a frilling stick into the wider end of the cone and open slightly and leave to dry. Repeat this process till you have three of each colour.

CRAB

7. Colour approx 30g of white modelling paste using the orange ProGel®. Roll into a ball shape and flatten slightly to give an oval shape body. With the small end of the cutting wheel, make a wide smiley mouth shape, then with the pointed end of the cel stick, indent at each end of the mouth. Just above, insert the cel stick twice for the nostrils. To make the back legs, roll out small thin sausage shapes, slightly pointed at one end (approx 15mm in length). Make six of these. Group these into 3's for either side of the crab body and secure in position using edible glue. For the front claws, make two small pea size balls and using edible glue attach to the front of body. Make two larger balls, cut with the small scissors at one end (approx 10mm) to create a claw shape. Attach to the front of the smaller balls of paste with edible glue and position on top of the cake. For the eyes, make two small balls using the white modelling paste. Colour a small amount of white modelling paste using the black ProGel®* and using a 6mm circle cutter, roll and cut out two pieces. Attach each one to the white balls of modelling paste with edible glue. To finish the eyes make two tiny balls of paste using the white modelling paste and attach to the black centre with edible glue.

OCTOPUS

8. Colour approx 50g of white modelling paste using the purple ProGel®. Make eight small thin sausage shapes and curl each at one end. Place on the board, securing with edible glue. With the remaining purple modelling paste, make a ball shape. Create a mouth (as you did with the crab). For the eyes use the same process as with the crab but using a 13mm and 10mm circle cutter. Attach body to the legs with edible glue.

MERMAID

9. Colour 40g of white modelling paste with peach ProGel®. For the head use 15g of peach modelling paste using the 4th largest head in the mould. Paint the eyes by mixing plain & simple, snowdrift with dipping solution and paint both ovals. Then with plain & simple, black magic mixed with dipping solution, paint the lower part of the eye. Dust the cheeks with edible silk, pearl blush pink and attach a nose using a tiny piece of peach paste. For the eye lashes and eye brows, use the thin nib of the black and the chocolate food pen once the head is dry.

10. Colour approx 100g of modelling paste using pink ProGel®. Roll into a sausage shape making thinner at one end to form the tail. Use edible glue to secure in place as per the main image. Place one or two of the rocks made earlier ,at the back of the tail end to support it. Roll out pink modelling paste and cut out the tail fin using the teardrop shape cutter, frilling the widest area with the frilling stick. Brush with edible glue to secure in position on the tail end. Still using the pink modelling paste, cut out the scales with the rose petal cutter and texture using the frilling stick. Attach in position on the tail with edible glue, point side up. Repeat this process until the whole tail has been covered. Save two small balls of pink modelling paste for the bikini top.

11. Using 20g of the peach modelling paste, roll into a small sausage shape to make the body and pinch in at the top end to shape the neck. Brush the top of the tail with edible glue and attach the body. With the cel stick make a belly button. Carefully push a wooden skewer through the neck, body and cake till it touches the cake drum board. Trim the skewer using wire cutters, leaving enough to attach the head.

12. For the arms, use 10g of peach modelling paste and roll into a thin sausage shape, cut in half and roll slightly thinner at one end to make the hands. Using small scissors, cut at the side edge to make the thumbs. With a small knife mark the fingers. Secure the arms using edible glue.

13. Using the small amount of pink modelling paste saved from earlier, make into small flattened cone shapes and attach to the front of the body for the bikini. Once the upper body has firmed slightly, attach the head with edible glue.

14. Colour approx 20g of white modelling paste using the brown ProGel®. Brush the top of the head with edible glue. Roll thin sausages of paste for the hair and attach to the head, creating a style as you go.

15. Attach the long leaves, rocks, shells, fish, flowers and corals to the cake using small amounts of royal icing. Once everything is secure mix white hologram glitter with dipping solution and paint over the tail, coral, fish and some of the shells to create a sparkling finish.

POP-Tastic!

Easy

YOU WILL NEED (FOR THE BASE)

- A batch of cake pop mix (See recipes at back of book)
- Cake pop sticks
- A shallow tin
- White candy melts
- ProGel®* - Cream
- Large star cutter (approx 5cm)
- Tiny oval cutter
- Edible Glitter*- Gold
- Edible Glue*
- Very small amount of pink, black and white flowerpaste

  * Rainbow Dust Colours products

METHOD

1. Press the cake pop mix into the shallow tin and place in the fridge to firm up. Once firm press out star shapes using the star cutter and push a stick into the base of each star. Put the stars back into the fridge until needed.

2. Melt the white candy melt as per the instructions and colour using the cream ProGel®. Take the stars from the fridge, dip each one into the candy melt allowing the excess to drip off and push the coated stars into a piece of oasis or a cake pop holder. Once the stars have just started to set but are still tacky, they can be sprinkled with edible gold glitter. Place back in the holder and store in the fridge to set.

3. Roll out the white flowerpaste and cut out two oval eyes for each star. Add a small ball of black flowerpaste for the centre of each eye. Roll the pink flowerpaste into a very thin sausage and make into circles and shapes to create various mouths. Take the stars from the fridge and attach the features with edible glue.

YOU WILL NEED (FOR THE PUSH POPS)

- Batch of Vanilla cake mix
- ProGel®*- Turquoise
- Sparkling Sugar Crystals*- Metallic Gold
- Batch of buttercream
- Large star nozzle and piping bag
- Push pop holders
- Circle cutter (the same size as your push pop holder)
- Selection of sea creatures
  (as made in the previous mermaid cake)

  * Rainbow Dust Colours products

METHOD

1. Colour the batch of cake mix with the turquoise ProGel®and bake in a shallow tin. Turn out and leave to cool, trimming all the edges from the sponge. This will reveal the true colour of the cake. Cut out circles from the sponge (we used 3 circles for each push pop). Push a circle of sponge into the push pop holder and top with a small swirl of buttercream, repeat two more times, making the top swirl extend above the push pop holder. Sprinkle with sugar crystals and top with a small sea creature.

2. We displayed the cake pops and push pops in a rectangular piece of polystyrene dummy which was covered to look like drift wood. We then added baby blue and metallic gold sugar crystals on the board for a sea and beach effect, finishing with coral, reeds and shells etc, as used on the mermaid cake.

Diamonds Are A Girls Best Friend!

Medium

YOU WILL NEED

- 5 inch (13cm) square cake
- 8 inch (20cm) square cake
- 2 x 5 inch (13cm) drum board
- 2 x 8 inch (20cm) drum board
- 14 inch (35.5cm) drum board
- 7 inch (18cm) and 10 inch (25.5) thin square boards to be used as template for the lids
- 3.250kg of white sugarpaste
- 400g of white flowerpaste
- ProGel®*- Turquoise and Pink
- Sparkle Range (Non-Toxic Glitter)*- White Hologram (you will need 2 pots), Silver Hologram (cupcakes only)
- Edible Silk Range*- Starlight Pink Sky
- Metallic Food Paint*- Pearl White
- Edible Glue*
- Edible Glitter* - White (cupcakes only)
- Strip cutter No. 5 (JEM)
- Royal icing ruler or template cut to a depth of 1 ¾ inch (35mm)
- Bead maker 6mm (HH)
- Five petal cutter (FMM) – 35mm, 75mm and 90mm
- Dove and hearts mould (FPC) (cupcakes only)
- 1M nozzle - Wilton (cupcakes only)
- Buttercream (we made this using white vegetable margarine)
- Royal Icing
- Sharp top edger (Edgers)
- Dowels
- Bone tool
- Cel pad
- Scroll textured rolling pin- cupcakes only (JEM)
- 2m of satin ribbon or diamanté strip

     * Rainbow Dust Colour products

METHOD

1. Using the white sugarpaste, cover the 14 inch drum board. Colour the remaining sugarpaste using the turquoise ProGel®. Using a small amount of royal icing, secure the two 8 inch drum boards together and place the 8 inch cake on top. Fill the cake and cover with buttercream. Roll out the turquoise sugarpaste and cover the cake, using the sharp top edger to finish the corners and edges (this will create a sharp edge effect). Repeat with the smaller cake.

2. Roll out the sugarpaste to approx 5mm and using the 7 inch thin board as a guide, cut out a square of sugarpaste and place over the top of the smaller cake. This will create the lid. Attach with edible glue and trim all the sides to a depth of approx 1 ¾ inch (35mm). Repeat with the large cake and leave to dry.

3. Using the white flowerpaste and the bead maker, make 4 lengths of beads, leaving them to dry in a curved position. They can be dusted with edible silk, pearl white.

4. To create the ribbon decoration, roll out the white flowerpaste to approx 3mm, rolling out a piece long enough to fit across the larger cake. Use the icing ruler (or your template) as a guide, cut out a strip of paste, brush with edible glue and sprinkle with white hologram glitter. Do this on a separate sheet of paper so the excess can be used again. Attach the strip to the cake, placing about 1 inch from the front and, repeat with the second strip, placing this across the first about 1 inch from the edge.

5. Repeat the same process for the smaller cake, placing these strips across the centre and leave to set on the cakes. Once firm, the cakes can then be dowelled and the top tier place onto the base cake at an angle.

6. Make the bows by rolling out white flowerpaste and using the strip cutter, cut out two pieces for each bow. Fold each piece in half, placing a piece of rolled up kitchen roll in the centre to keep the bow open until it is dry. Pinch the end together, this will give the bow a slightly ruched and more natural look. Secure the 2 ends together in the centre with edible glue and leave to dry.

7. Using the icing ruler (or your template), cut out 4 pieces for the tails of the bows, cutting a 'V' at one end of each piece. Glitter all the pieces and attach in position on the cakes. Once the bows are completely dry, brush with edible glue and sprinkle with white hologram glitter, shaking off the excess. Attach these pieces to the cake with royal icing, placing small balls of paste behind each bow to raise them slightly. Once in position, cut another strip of flowerpaste for the centre of the bow using the strip cutter. Cut in half, glitter and slightly ruche. Attach across the centre of each bow tucking in the edges.

8. For the roses, colour the remaining flowerpaste with the pink ProGel®, roll out thinly and cut three 35mm 5 petal flowers. Place the petal onto the cel pad and using the bone tool, thin all the edges to create movement. Make a small ball of pink flowerpaste and attach to the centre of the petal with a small amount of edible glue. Apply edible glue to the petals and fold each petal around the ball. Continue with two more petals until you have a small open rose. Make two of these flowers and repeat the same process to make the two larger roses using three 75mm petals and three 90mm petals. Leave to dry in a flower former or a piece of kitchen foil which has been moulded into a small dish shape and leave to dry.

9. Dust each rose with the edible silk, pearl pink sky. Arrange the roses and pearls on the cake, securing with royal icing. Finish the edge of the board using a diamanté strip or satin ribbon.

It's All In The Detail

MATCHING CUPCAKES (2 DESIGNS)

1. Make the small roses and the pearls the same way as those in the main cake. Take one strip of pearls and make a circle to fit your cupcake, leave to dry and dust with edible silk, pearl white.

2. Using the dove and hearts mould, make a small heart for each pearl bracelet you have made. Leave to dry and then glitter using the silver hologram.

3. Roll out pink flowerpaste and emboss using the scroll rolling pin, cut out discs slightly smaller than the cupcake you are using and leave to dry. Brush the discs with edible silk, pearl pink sky.

4. Using the white buttercream in a bag with the 1M nozzle, pipe ruffles into a peak for the cakes that require a rose. Sprinkle with white edible glitter and place a rose on top.

5. For the bracelet cupcakes, colour the remaining buttercream with the turquoise ProGel® and using the 1M tube again pipe a ruffle circle on the cakes. Place a pink disc on the top of each cake, attaching a bracelet and a heart with royal icing.

Parade Of The Monsters

Medium

YOU WILL NEED (THE MOON CAKE)

- 16 inch (40.5cm) Square drum board
- 8 inch (20cm) Half ball shaped cake
- 2.750kg of white sugarpaste
- ProGel®*- Black and Yellow
- 30g Edible Glitter*- Yellow
- Edible Glue*
- Brush
- Edible Silver Stars*
- 2m of Black 15mm satin ribbon

* Rainbow Dust Colour products

METHOD

1. Colour 1.5kg of white sugarpaste with black ProGel®, cover the board and leave to dry.

2. Colour 1.25kg of white sugarpaste with yellow ProGel®. Make 4 doughnut shaped pieces and 3 flattened balls. Attach to the cake using edible glue. This will help form the craters and bumps on the moon.

3. Coat the entire cake with buttercream. Roll out the remaining sugarpaste and cover the cake on a separate board, smoothing round all the craters and bumps with your fingers.

4. Once the moon cake is dry, brush over the entire cake with edible glue. Sprinkle yellow edible glitter over the whole cake. Once you are happy with the finish, place the cake on a separate board and leave to dry.

5. Place the cake in position on the board that has been covered in black sugarpaste, securing with buttercream. Decorate the black base with silver stars.

YOU WILL NEED (MONSTER 1 - SPIKE)

- ProGel®*- Mint Green, Tangerine, Purple and Black
- 100g of white sugarpaste
- Tylo powder*
- Small circle cutter
- Quilting tool
- Cel stick
- Edible Glue*
- Small palette knife

* Rainbow Dust Colour products

METHOD

1. Colour 70g of white sugarpaste using the mint green ProGel®, 15g tangerine, 5g black, 5g purple, leaving the remaining 5g white. Add a small amount of tylo powder to firm the paste.

2. Using 45g of mint green sugarpaste, mould into a ball and mark the mouth using the quilting tool, marking at the edges of the mouth with the cel stick.

3. For the feet, take 15g of mint green, form into a ball and cut in half. Roll each piece into a cone shape, flattening the narrow end. Place the flattened ends together and attach the body with edible glue. Make three small holes in the end of each foot to attach the toes.

4. To make the hands, use ⅔ of the remaining green paste. Forming a cone, mark the rounded end with the small palette knife to resemble the fingers.

5. Make a nose with the remaining paste, marking the nostrils with the end of the cel stick.

6. Using the tangerine sugarpaste, make two small balls for the eyes, flatten into an oval shape and attach with edible glue. With a small amount of tangerine sugarpaste, make tiny pointed cones for the claws and using edible glue, insert into the holes on the feet. Make eight pointed cones for the spikes and attach to the side of the body.

7. Using a small ball of flattened white sugarpaste, attach to the eyes and then add a smaller ball of black sugarpaste for the centres. Finish with two small pointed sausages of purple sugarpaste, attaching in place for the eyebrows.

YOU WILL NEED (MONSTER 2 TUNNEL VISION TINA)

- ProGel®*- Tangerine, Purple and Black
- Tylo Powder*
- Edible Glue*
- Small diamond cutter
- 85g of white sugarpaste
- 20mm and 15mm circle cutter
- Cel stick
- Dresden tool
- Wooden skewer

* Rainbow Dust Colour products

METHOD

1. Add a small amount of tylo powder to firm the sugarpaste. Using the ProGel®, take the white sugarpaste and colour 70g tangerine, 10g purple and 2g black, leaving the remainder white.

2. Form 60g of tangerine paste into a small chunky sausage shape, making one end slightly thinner and make the base flat. Push a skewer into the cake where you would like your character to sit, cutting off to the approx length of the sausage. Attach the sausage over the skewer, with a small amount of edible glue. Create a mouth using the dresden tool, marking the corners of the mouth with the cel stick. Make the arm from the remaining 10g of tangerine sugarpaste, forming into a flattened sausage and marking the fingers with the dresden tool. Cut at an angle and attach to the body with edible glue.

3. Roll out the white sugarpaste and cut out a circle using the 20mm cutter, attach to the centre of the monsters head. Roll out the purple paste and cut a 15mm circle, attaching to the centre of the white circle. To finish, cut out a black diamond for the centre of the eye.

4. Roll the remaining purple paste into four thin sausages and attach to the head for the hair.

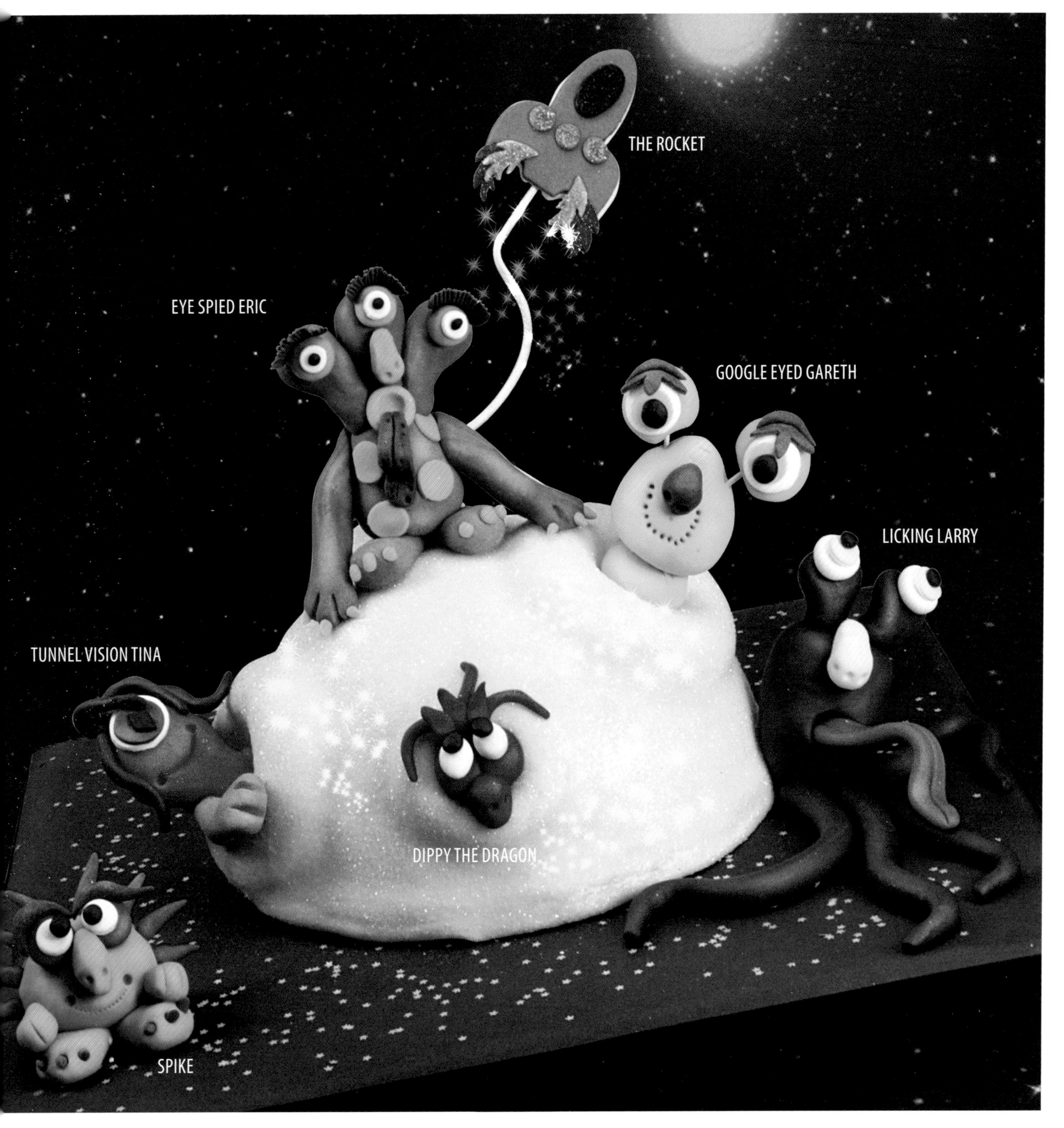

THE ROCKET

EYE SPIED ERIC

GOOGLE EYED GARETH

LICKING LARRY

TUNNEL VISION TINA

DIPPY THE DRAGON

SPIKE

YOU WILL NEED (MONSTER 3 EYE SPIED ERIC)

- ProGel®*- Ice Blue, Mint Green, Purple and Black
- Tylo Powder*
- Edible Glue*
- 120g of white sugarpaste
- 10mm and 15mm circle cutter
- 40mm oval cutter
- Small pair of scissors
- Cel stick
- Wooden skewer
- 3 cocktail sticks

* Rainbow Dust Colour products

METHOD

1. Add a small amount of tylo powder to firm up the paste. Using the ProGel® colour 100g of sugarpaste Ice blue, 10g mint green, 5g purple and 2g black, leaving the remaining piece white. Using 40g of ice blue paste, form into a small chunky sausage, approx 40mm in length, rounding off the ends. With approx 5g of ice blue paste, divide and form into two cones for the feet, making one end thinner than the other. Attach the feet onto the cake in the position required and secure with edible glue. Push the wooden skewer into the cake where the backs of the feet are touching, then push the body onto the skewer, securing with edible glue.

2. Make two long arms using 15g of ice blue sugarpaste, divided into two and roll each piece into a long sausage. Make one end slightly more rounded, pinching in at the wrist. Cut the top of each arm at an angle and attach to the body with edible glue.

3. Using the mint green sugarpaste, make 12 tiny spiked cones, attaching 3 onto the ends of the feet and the arms. Roll out and cut 7, 15mm circles and attach to the body. Using the remaining ice blue paste, divide into 3 and form into long pear shapes. Push the narrower end onto a cocktail stick and push into the centre of the body with one shape at either side, securing with edible glue.

4. Make 3 small balls of mint green sugarpaste, flatten and attach to the tops of each pear shape. Make a nose in the shape of a small pear, marking the nostrils with the cel stick. Attach under the central eye and make the mouth using a flattened ball of paste and pushing your finger into the centre to make an opening. Attach under the nose.

5. Cut 3 10mm circles from the white sugarpaste and place in the centre of the green eyes, finish with a small black centre. To make the eyelashes, roll out the purple paste and cut 2 oval shapes. Cut into the shapes to form the lashes and attach to the tops of the eyes.

6. With the remaining purple paste roll into a long sausage and flatten. Attach into the mouth, marking a centre line with the dresden tool.

YOU WILL NEED (MONSTER 4 GOOGLE EYED GARETH)

- ProGel®*- Lime Green, Purple and Black
- 105g of white sugarpaste
- Wooden skewer
- 2 cocktail sticks
- Cel stick
- Tylo Powder*
- Edible Glue*
- Small calyx cutter

METHOD

1. Add a small amount of tylo powder to firm up the paste. Using the ProGel® colour 90g of sugarpaste lime green, 5g purple, 5g black leaving the remaining 5g white. Using 10g of lime green sugarpaste, form a ball, flatten slightly and position on cake, securing with edible glue. Push the wooden skewer through the centre of the ball and the cake.

2. Using 70g of lime green sugarpaste, form into a triangle shape and push onto the skewer, attaching with edible glue. Mark a smiling mouth using the cel stick. Push in the two cocktail sticks at either side of the head, and using the rest of the lime green sugarpaste (leaving a small amount for the centres of the eyes) form into two flattened balls. Push each ball onto the ends of the cocktail sticks.

3. Make two flattened balls of white sugarpaste and attach to the eyes, followed with a smaller piece of lime green sugarpaste and finished with a black centre. Roll out the purple sugarpaste and cut out a calyx. Cut in half and attach the pieces to the tops of the eyes and finish with a small purple sausage. Use a small triangle shaped nose and mark the nostrils using a cel stick.

YOU WILL NEED (MONSTER 5 - LICKING LARRY)

- ProGel®*- Purple, Yellow, Tangerine and Black
- 200g of white sugarpaste
- Tylo Powder*
- Edible Glue*
- Dresden tool, cel stick
- 10mm circle cutter
- 2 cocktail sticks

METHOD

1. Add a small amount of tylo powder to firm up the paste. Using the ProGel® colour 185g of white sugarpaste purple, 5g Yellow and 5g tangerine, leaving the remaining 5g white. Using 70g of purple sugarpaste, form a rounded oblong shape, pushing your finger into the bottom half to form the mouth. Attach in position at the side of the cake with a edible glue. Divide 100g of purple paste into 5 pieces. Roll each piece into long pointed tentacles, attaching with edible glue from the body onto the board and place each tentacle at different angles.

2. Using purple sugarpaste, make 2 pear shapes for the eye sockets and attach to the top of the head with the cocktail sticks. Make 2 flattened balls of white sugarpaste for the eyeballs, add 2 yellow circles and finish with a black centre. With the remaining yellow paste, form into a pear

shaped nose, attach to the face and mark nostrils with the cel stick. Make the tongue by rolling the tangerine paste into a flat sausage, marking down the centre with the dresden tool. Attach to the mouth.

YOU WILL NEED (MONSTER 6 DIPPY THE DRAGON)

- ProGel®*- Red and Black
- Cel stick
- 25g of white sugarpaste
- Tylo Pwder*

METHOD

1. Using the ProGel®, colour 20g of sugarpaste red and half of the remaining piece black, leaving a small piece white. Using 10g of red sugarpaste, divide into 3, make two of the pieces into flattened oval shapes and the third into a pear shape. Attach the pieces into the centre of the moon crater, with the two flattened oval pieces at the top and the pear shapes piece underneath, making the nose. Mark three nostrils with the cel stick.

2. Make two small oval pieces from white paste and attach to the centres of the eyes, finishing with a small ball of black sugarpaste.

3. With the remaining red sugarpaste, make 3 long sausages and 3 long pointed cones, attaching these to the top of the head.

THE ROCKET

- Cookie dough (see recipe in back of book)
- Rocket cookie cutter (BSA)
- 20g of white flowerpaste
- ProGel®*- Ice Blue, Purple, Tangerine and Red
- Edible Glue*
- Edible Glitter- Purple, Orange and Red
- 2 x 20# florist wires & white florist tape
- 40mm oval cutter
- 10mm circle cutter
- Fire shape cutter
- Small posy pick

METHOD

1. Roll out the cookie dough and cut out the rocket. Wrap together the florist wires with florist tape. Wrap the wire around a small rolling pin to form a loose coil, flattening off one end slightly so it can be pushed into the base of the cookie. Bake and leave to cool.

2. Colour 10g of flowerpaste using ice blue ProGel®. Roll and cut out a rocket. Attach the paste to the cookie with edible glue. Divide the remaining flowerpaste into 3 and colour with red, purple and tangerine ProGel®. Roll out each colour and cut out 3 small tangerine circles, 2 tangerine flames, 2 red flames and 1 purple oval. Brush each piece with edible glue, sprinkle with the co-ordinating edible glitter and attach the pieces to the rocket as pictured. Place a small piece of flowerpaste into the small posy pick and push in the cookies wire. The posy pick can then be placed in position on the cake.

MONSTER COOKIES!

Make the monster cookies by using a selection of shaped cookie cutters and insert them onto long lolly sticks before baking. Decorate using the same techniques from the main cake tutorial.

Eye Spy With My Many Eyes.....

YOU WILL NEED

- 12 long lolly sticks
- Approx 50g of white sugarpaste
- 3 small circle cutters
- White candy melt
- Green candy melt
- 1 batch of cake pop mix (see recipe section at back of book)
- ProGel®*- Black and Lime Green
- Sparkling Sugar Crystals*- Pearlescent Green
- Edible Shapes - Dark silver stars
- Edible Glue*

   *Rainbow Dust Colour products

METHOD

1. Divide the cake pop mix into 12 equal pieces and roll into balls. Push a stick into each ball and freeze on the sticks until firm.

2. Melt the candy melts as per the manufacturers instructions. Once the balls are firm dip each one into the white candy melt and leave to set. Once set, dip each one only half way into the green candy melt, leave until tacky and sprinkle with the sugar crystals. Leave to set.

3. Divide the white sugarpaste into 3. Using the ProGel®, colour one piece black, one lime green and leave the remaining piece white. Roll out the white sugarpaste and using the largest circle cutter, cut out a disc for each cake pop. Repeat using the medium circle cutter with the lime green sugarpaste and the smallest circle cutter with the black paste.

4. Attach the white discs to the cake pop with edible glue, then the lime green and finishing with the black. We displayed the cake pop eyes in a square glass vase, filled with lime green jelly (this has been made up using less water to make a much firmer jelly) and sprinkled with green sugar crystals.

5. Make the arms, nose and mouth with sugarpaste and attach them to the vase with edible glue. Once the jelly has set, arrange the cake pops in the vase.

6. To add a finishing touch, sprinkle the base with the dark silver stars.

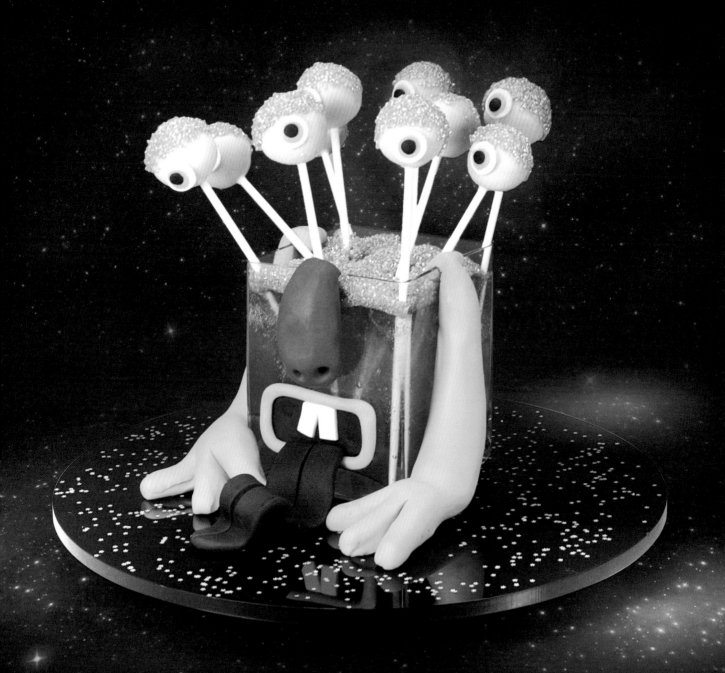

Blossoms & Butterflies

Easy

YOU WILL NEED

- 12 cupcakes
- 500g of white sugarpaste
- 200g of white flowerpaste
- 12 Butterfly design cake wrappers
- Metallic Dark Gold Food Paint*
- Sparkle Range (Non-Toxic Glitter)- Fire Red Glitter*
- Click-Twist Brush®- Dark Gold
- Edible Glue*
- ProGel®*- Cream and Red
- Butterfly Trio mould (FPC)
- Small and medium blossom plunger cutter
- Royal icing in a bag with a No. 1 tube
- Buttercream
- Large paint brush
- 12 pieces of red tissue paper cut into 18cm squares
- Circle cutter (the same size of the top of your cupcake)
- Cupcake box that holds 12

    * Rainbow Dust Colour products

METHOD

1. Divide the flowerpaste in half and colour one half with red ProGel® and the other half with cream ProGel®. Using the butterfly mould, make 4 large and 8 medium red butterflies and 4 large cream butterflies. Leave to dry.

2. Once the butterflies are dry, brush the red ones with edible glue and sprinkle with fire red glitter. Leave to dry. Paint the cream ones using the dark gold Click-Twist Brush® and leave to dry.

3. Using red flowerpaste, cut out 32 medium and 20 small blossoms, repeat using the cream flowerpaste. Once the cream ones are dry, paint using the dark gold Click-Twist Brush®.

4. Paint both sides of the cake wrappers using the metallic dark gold food paint and leave to dry.

5. To assemble, make sure that all the cupcakes are level. Roll out the white sugarpaste to approx 5mm thickness and cut out 12 discs. Secure the discs to the top of each cupcake with buttercream.

DESIGN 1

1. Attach 8 gold and 8 red medium blossoms around the edge of 4 of the cupcakes using royal icing. Finish the centres of the blossoms with a small dot of royal icing and attach a large red butterfly to the centre of each cupcake.

DESIGN 2

1. Pipe 2 swirls of royal icing on either side of 4 cupcakes and leave to set. Once set paint the swirl using the dark gold Click-Twist Brush®. Attach a red and gold butterfly on either side of the cupcake. Place a small red and gold blossom on each swirl.

DESIGN 3

1. Pipe 8 swirls from the centre of the remaining 4 cakes and leave to set. Paint with the dark gold Click-Twist Brush® and attach 4 red and 4 gold blossoms to the ends of the swirls. Finishing each cake with a medium red butterfly.

2. Assemble the cupcake box. Make up the painted gold cake wrappers and place a cake in each one . Place a piece of red tissue over a cupcake hole then push in the cake and wrapper, bringing the tissue up the sides. Repeat with each cake. Finish with a bow if you wish.

Who's For Caketails?

YOU WILL NEED

MOJITO

- Sponge mix
- Mojito flavour (Beau products)
- Lime jelly
- Sparkling Sugar Crystals*- Pearlescent White
- Mint leaves and lime slice
- White rum
- Small glasses

* Rainbow Dust Colour products

TEQUILA SUNRISE

- Sponge mix
- ProGel®*- Red and Orange
- Tequila sunrise flavour (Beau products)
- Strawberry (or any red jelly) (2 packs depending on how many and the size of your cocktails)
- Double cream (small pot)
- Small amount of mandarin orange segments (chopped)
- Orange slice and umbrella for decoration
- Small glasses

* Rainbow Dust Colour products

PINA COLODA

- Sponge mix
- Pineapple jelly
- Pina Colada flavour (Beau products)
- ProGel®*- Lemon
- Double cream for the tops
- Fresh pineapple diced finely
- Fresh pineapple slice and a cocktail cherry
- Small glass
- White rum

* Rainbow Dust Colour products

METHOD

1. Flavour the sponge mix with the mojito flavour and bake in cupcake cases, leave to cool.

2. Make the lime jelly as per the instructions, adding a small amount of white rum (leave out some of the water and add the rum). Pour the jelly into the glasses, leaving approx 2cm at the top of the glass. Place the jelly into the fridge until it has just started to set.

3. Trim the crust off the cupcake and cut into 1cm cubes. Push the cubes into the partially set jelly, putting in as much or as little as you like. Place the jelly back in the fridge to set firm.

4. When ready to serve, top each glass with the white sugar crystals to resemble crushed ice. Decorate with a sprig of mint and a slice of fresh lime.

METHOD

1. Split the sponge mix in half, colour one half with red ProGel® and the other using the orange ProGel®. Flavouring both with the tequila sunrise flavour and mix both colours lightly together to make a marble effect sponge. Bake in cupcake cases and leave to cool.

2. Make up the red jelly as per instructions and pour into the glasses, only filling ⅓ of the glass and leave to set in the fridge.

3. Whip the cream and add the chopped mandarin orange segments. Store in the fridge until needed.

4. Trim the crusts off the sponge cakes and slice into slices ½ cm deep and approx 3-4 cm long. Place all the sponge slices around the glass, pressing them together. Fill the centre cavity with the the orange cream mix and top with a thin circle of sponge. Place in the fridge to firm.

5. Using the remaining red jelly, which has cooled but not set, fill the glasses to the top. Leave to set in the fridge. Decorate with slices of orange and a cocktail umbrella.

METHOD

1. Colour the sponge mix using the lemon ProGel® and add the pina colada flavouring. Bake in cupcake cases and leave to cool.

2. Make up the pineapple jelly and add a little white rum. Making the volume of water no more than instructed.

3. Trim the crusts off the sponge cakes and slice into 1cm circles. Place a circle of sponge in the base of a glass, soak with jelly and leave to set. Top with chopped pineapple. Then add another layer of sponge and once more soak with jelly. Leave to set then top with pineapple. Whip the cream and fill the remaining space to the top of the glass and smooth off level with a knife.

4. Decorate with a slice of pineapple and a cocktail cherry.

* Please note that using fresh pineapple with the jelly will create a softer setting dessert.

MOJITO   **TEQUILA SUNRISE**   **PINA COLODA**

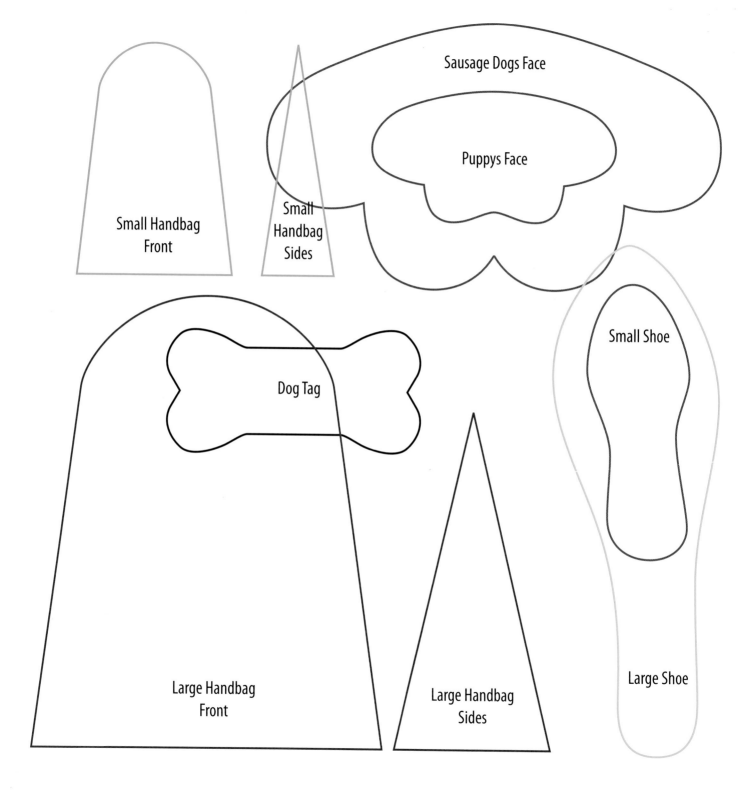

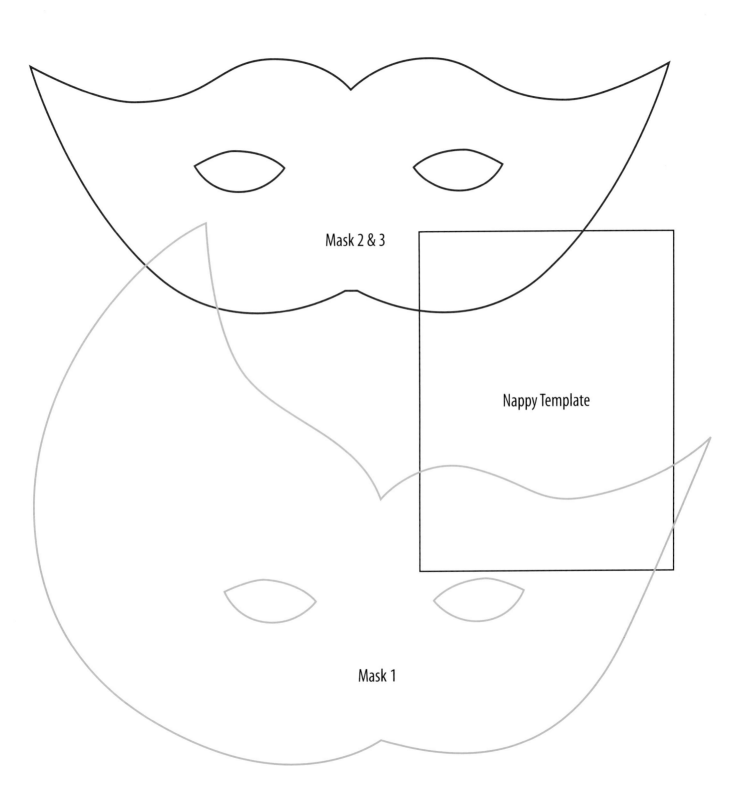

Mask 2 & 3

Nappy Template

Mask 1

RECIPES

CAKE POP RECIPE

Makes 12 large or 24 small cake pops

280g Cake Crumbs
160g Buttercream
Lolly Sticks

Put the cake crumbs into a bowl and mix in the buttercream, form the mix into a ball using your hands.
Divide the mix into the amount of cake pops you require and form into balls. Push each pop onto a stick and freeze until firm. Once firm they can be decorated.

COOKIE DOUGH

Makes about 20 cookies
Oven temp 180c, 160 fan, gas 4

180g Butter
180g Caster Sugar
1 Egg
400g Plain Flour

In a mixer cream butter and sugar until well mixed.
Beat in the egg and add the flour. Mix until it forms a ball.
Place in fridge for approx 45 mins to rest.
Roll out on a floured surface to a 5mm thickness.
Cut out the required shapes and place onto a lined baking tray and chill again for approx 20 mins.
Bake for 8-10 mins until golden brown.

MODELLING PASTE

225g sifted icing sugar
1 tbs Tylo powder*
30ml cold water

*Rainbow Dust Colour product

For best results make this mix using a food mixer.
Put all the ingredients into a bowl and combine together into a ball.
Store in a sealed bag.

ROYAL ICING

600g Sifted icing sugar
3x Egg whites

Place the egg whites into a bowl and mix until combined. Add the icing sugar and once combined, beat until the icing is glossy. The icing can be kept for 2-3 days in a sealed container or in a bowl covered with a damp clean tea towel, making sure that the towel is always damp or the icing will crust over.

RICE KRISPIE CAKE

200g Rice Krispies
200g Marshmallows
120g Butter
220g Toffees

Melt the butter and toffees together. Add the marshmallows and mix well until they have melted. Then add the Rice Krispies and stir until all the ingredients are combined. Place into a greased tin (25cm x 20cm) or mould.

HOW TO TEMPER CHOCOLATE

Small chocolate buttons
Thermometer
Wooden spoon
Plastic mixing bowl

Melt ¾ of the chocolate buttons gently, to a temperature of 45c.
Add the remaining chocolate and stir until the temperature has dropped to 33c/34c.
Rest for approx 5 minutes, give a final stir and the chocolate is ready to use.

Useful Contacts

BLOSSOM SUGAR ART (BSA)
Dalton House, 60 Windsor Ave, London, SW192RR
Tel: 02036000198
www.blossomsugarart.com

DIAMOND PASTE (DP)
78 Battle Road, St Leonards-on-Sea, E. Sussex, TN37 7AG
Tel: 01424 432448
www.sugarcity.co.uk

EDGERS
2 Moss Crescent, Meadowfield Park Estate
Crawcrook, Tyne & Wear
NE40 4XL
Tel: 0756 535 3714
www.edgers.co.uk

FMM SUGARCRAFT (FMM)
Unit 7, Chancerygate Business Park, Whiteleaf Road
Hemel Hempstead, Herts, HP3 9HD
Tel: 01442 292970
www.fmmsugarcraft.com

FPC SUGARCRAFT (FPC)
Hillview, Parfitts, Bristol, BS5 8BN
Tel: 01179853249
www.fpcsugarcraft.co.uk

HAWTHORNE HILL (HH)
Suite 8A, Northern Diver Building.
Appley Lane North, Appley Bridge,
Wigan, Lancashire. WN6 9AE
Tel: 07905 811505
www.hawthornehill.co.uk

JEM
Unit 21, Riverwalk Rd, Enfield EN37QN
Tel: 02032340049
www.cakedecoration.co.uk

KAREN DAVIES SUGARCRAFT LTD (KD)
Unit 4, Royal Standard House, 330-334 New Chester Rd,
Birkenhead, Merseyside, CH42 1LE
Tel: 0151 643 0055
www.karendaviescakes.co.uk

ORCHARD PRODUCTS UK LTD (OP)
149 Hook Road, Surbiton, London KT6 7AR
Tel: 020 8391 4668
www.orchardsugarart.co.uk

SILVERWOOD - ALAN SILVERWOOD LIMITED (SW)
Ledsam House, Ledsam Street, Birmingham, B16 8DN
Tel: 0121 454 3571
www.alansilverwood.co.uk

STEPHEN BENISON (SB)
28 Rodwell Park, Trowbridge, Wiltshire, BA14 7LY
Tel: 01225 768649
www.sugar-artistry.co.uk

WE WOULD LIKE TO SAY A SPECIAL THANK YOU TO **FPC SUGARCRAFT** AND **BLOSSOM SUGAR ART** WHO KINDLY SUPPORTED OUR PROJECTS WITH THEIR FANTASTIC PRODUCTS. BOTH MANUFACTURING COMPANIES ARE VERY ACTIVE WITHIN THE CURRENT CAKE DECORATING MARKET AND ARE SOME OF THE FRIENDLIEST PEOPLE YOU COULD WISH TO DEAL WITH. THANK YOU ONCE AGAIN!

FPC SUGARCRAFT (FPC)
Hillview, Parfitts, Bristol, BS5 8BN
Tel: 01179853249
www.fpcsugarcraft.co.uk

BLOSSOM SUGAR ART (BSA)
Dalton House, 60 Windsor Ave, London, SW192RR
Tel: 02036000198
www.blossomsugarart.com

Quick Product Guide

SPARKLE RANGE GLITTERS

They are the brightest colours on the market and bounce light off their surface to great effect! With over 70 colours in this range, they have a magnitude of uses within cake decorating.

The most common use for the Sparkle Range glitters is to apply them (using Rainbow Dust Colours, edible glue) to sugar shapes (e.g. sugar hearts on wires), for use on cake toppers or cupcake decorations. They are also very popular as a decorative trimming on sugar flowers and even adding a dazzling sparkle to a cake board. These are just a few examples of how the cake decorating community uses these glitters to great effect.

EDIBLE SILK RANGE LUSTRE POWDERS

These powders are best applied using a dry brush technique. When applying, use a suitable sized brush for the size of area you need to cover. Lustre dust can also be used as a paint by mixing a small amount of dipping solution with the powder until the required consistency is achieved. Do not mix the lustre dust with water to make a paint as water will dissolve the icing.

PLAIN & SIMPLE MATT POWDERS

These powders are used much in the same way as the "Edible Silk Range" but the result is a matt finish (rather than a metallic one).

Matt dusts can also be used as a paint by mixing a small amount of dipping solution with the dust until the required consistency is achieved. It can be used thinner for painting onto cakes to achieve a water colour look.

Do not mix the lustre dust with water to make a paint as it will not mix correctly and go lumpy.

THE CLICK-TWIST BRUSHES®

Simply twist the end cap of the brush until the paint fills the tip and you're ready to go! When not in use, simply wipe any excess paint from the tip of the brush and place the cap back on until next time. No mess, no fuss. It's quick and easy!

For use when you're only working on a small area of detail or to help you achieve a fast and smooth working environment.

This is great for areas of small coverage and detail work thanks to the controlled delivery of paint into the brush tip. There is minimal wastage which means your Click-Twist Brush® is very economical, allowing you to paint many decorations!